UNDERSTANDING AGE

Social welfare and change

Liz Jeffery

First published in Great Britain in 2011 by

The Policy Press
University of Bristol
Fourth Floor
Beacon House
Queen's Road
Bristol BS8 1QU
UK

t: +44 (0)117 331 4054
f: +44 (0)117 331 4093
tpp-info@bristol.ac.uk
www.policypress.co.uk

North American office:
The Policy Press
c/o International Specialized Books Services
920 NE 58th Avenue, Suite 300
Portland, OR 97213-3786, USA
t: +1 503 287 3093
f: +1 503 280 8832
info@isbs.com

© The Policy Press 2011

British Library Cataloguing in Publication Data
A catalogue record for this book is available from the British Library.

Library of Congress Cataloging-in-Publication Data
A catalog record for this book has been requested.

ISBN 978 1 84742 330 6 paperback
ISBN 978 1 84742 331 3 hardcover

Cover design by The Policy Press.
Front cover: image kindly supplied by www.istock.com
Printed and bound in Great Britain by TJ International, Padstow.
The Policy Press uses environmentally responsible print partners.

FSC
www.fsc.org
MIX
Paper from
responsible sources
FSC® C013056

Contents

List of practice examples

Glossary of terms

Binary thinking The practice of thinking in terms of opposites (such as black or white; fat or thin) and not allowing for different shades of meaning.

Co-production The practice in which both paid professionals and service-users contribute their ideas to the development of public services.

Determinism The idea that every situation or event, including human action, is determined by previous causes.

Dialectic Arriving at a conclusion through a continuing process of conflict and of question and answer.

Discourse The use of language, together with signs and symbols, and its relation to social interaction.

Functionalism A social theory which suggests that the function, or intended function of an object or system, should or does take precedence over its form. Functionalism emphasises how different functions come together to form a coherent whole.

Narrative (identity, theory and therapy) Approaches that assume that there is no single truth or account of events, but that reality is constructed through social interaction. They take the view that each individual is the expert in his or her own life.

Postmodernism A reaction against the assumed certainty of scientific knowledge. Instead, postmodernism suggests that there is no one overarching way of interpreting the world, but that all truths are plural and relative.

Praxis A term referring to human action which emphasises its transformative nature and the significance of reflecting on one's actions.

Reflexivity The practice of considering one's actions on a continuing basis; a dynamic, continuing self-awareness which takes account of how one's own values and interests influence our behaviour.

Social pedagogy An educational term which refers to education in its widest and most holistic sense and which often straddles both the educational and social aspects of teaching.

Structuration theory A social theory that attempts to do justice to the idea of human action while also acknowledging the importance of societal structures.

'The other' An example of *binary thinking* in which the self is viewed in relation to an 'other' individual or group and where the latter is usually viewed in an antagonistic and hierarchical relationship to the self.

Transformative potential The capability that all individuals possess to intervene in a course of events (and hence to influence them) or to refrain from doing so.

Acknowledgements

I am indebted to Bob Ashcroft, whose lectures on the MA course in Bradford in the early 1990s introduced me to the ideas contained in this book. I would particularly like to thank Nick Frost and Terry Thomas, who have given so generously of their professorial knowledge and authorial experience over many a lunch hour and given me consistently helpful feedback and support. I am also grateful to Dave Gilbert for rescuing me at various times when I have had computer crises.

This book is dedicated to a number of friends who have supported me throughout, particularly Jeannette, Nigel and Louise, and my fellow members of the 'women's philosophy group', Angela, Barbara, Bron and Jo. I hope this book will prompt some lively discussions!

Acknowledgement

Introduction

Individual agency has attracted continuing interest in the last half-century. It emerged as a concept from sociology and social philosophy and, until quite recently, attention has focused on its contribution to theoretical debates, or in its perceived application to the varying fields of economics, management and foreign policy analysis (Carsnaes, 1992; Hendry, 1997; Sen, 1999a). More recently there has been growing academic debate about its relevance to social policy (Deacon and Mann, 1999; Williams, 1999; Hoggett, 2001) but probably only in the last ten years has much attention been paid to it within the literature relating specifically to social work and welfare.

Where agency's relevance has been recognised in social work, this has been implicit rather than explicit, a voice from the sidelines so to speak, rather than the key player (Parton and O'Byrne, 2000; Ferguson, 2003). This is surprising. Agency theory, with its inherent focus on the relationship between individuals and society, and on how societal and personal change is achieved is, arguably, the key issue in understanding the marginal position occupied by those with whom social welfare professionals engage, and how their movement from the periphery of society to a more central position can best be achieved.

The intention of this book is to bring individual agency in from the margins, to demonstrate how it is, whether we recognise it or not, a central fact of our societal existence. Acquiring an understanding of how it operates, its processes and its potential for achieving change, is therefore, arguably, crucial for those involved in the field of social welfare. It is a means of empowering them to become better, more effective practitioners so that they can, in turn, help those with whom they work to discover and exercise their own agency to positive effect. Potentially, agency theory provides a means of reinvigorating professional practice and theorising change. It offers, moreover, an important means of countering the obsession with measurement, targets and outcomes that currently bedevils the profession.

I will therefore be attempting critically to explore, examine and explain the concept of human agency as it has emerged from sociological literature, and to identify how it can help explicitly to recast social welfare theory and influence practice, specifically as a means of theorising and ultimately achieving change. In doing so, emphasis will be placed on drawing out the relevance of agency theory to current popular concepts and approaches within the field, such as 'empowerment', 'resilience' and the focus on 'narrative' and strengths – and solution-based practices. I will try to indicate how these ideas and practices flow directly from the concept of individual human agency that underlies them all and an understanding of which is therefore of central importance.

Chapter One will explore the concept of human agency, its emergence within the literature and how it has been theorised within the fields of sociology and social policy. Its progress within the frameworks of both sociology and psychology will be charted and how it has been developed, from classical theory through Marxism, feminism and post-modernism. The key influence of Giddens and his theory of the dynamic relationship between structure and agency and of agency's transformative potential will be outlined. How Giddens' ideas have been taken up and further developed in the last twenty years will be considered, tracing the major theoretical debates that have influenced social welfare since the founding of the welfare state, from the early focus on moral and religious concerns, right up to present-day practice. This chapter will conclude by asserting that an apparent synthesis is emerging between the current theoretical debate about human agency on the one hand and the issues and concerns now represented in social work literature.

Chapter Two explores how an understanding of human agency can usefully inform interventions with those who are users of services. A wide range of practices and methods such as personal construct psychology, solution-focused approaches, narrative therapy and self-help groups will be drawn on to indicate that, underlying all these approaches, is a commitment to promoting individual agency. It is suggested that an informed understanding of agency theory will help social welfare professionals to adopt appropriate practices and to develop new skills in working with service users.

In Chapter Three, consideration will be given to how users themselves can shape and control the services they use. In addition to focusing on areas of current practice, such as direct payments and the emphasis on participation, this chapter will explore what philosophical and political assumptions might lie behind these developments and how an exploration of power relations can illuminate the relationships concerned. Even in situations of acute distress and apparent powerlessness such as terminal illness, possibilities for the exercise of individual agency remain, and can leave those affected with a degree of control and dignity over the manner of their dying.

Chapter Four will involve exploration of human agency in a broader context and will focus on how individuals can collectively use their agency as members of communities and of wider societies. The potential for influencing the broader political agenda will be examined, drawing on the influence and practice, in different contexts of, for example, Fanon, Freire and Sen (Fanon, 1965; Freire, 1970; Sen, 1999a, 1999b). The potential of 'virtual' communities of interest, now offered through the internet will be addressed. Finally, the inherent uncertainty and unpredictability associated with agentic action and the possibility of unintended structural consequences will be considered, together with the associated potential irony of this for any government supposedly committed to promoting user-involvement but unhappy with what might emerge from so doing.

In conclusion, a case will be made out for welfare practices that are both more reflexive and responsive to service-users' needs, and at the same time more aware of their own limitations; and for the need for professionals to 'tread lightly', allowing more opportunity for service-users to shape their own futures in line with their personal identified agendas. In this context, services need to be less centrally controlled and prescriptive and freer to evolve according to expressed need.

Ultimately, it is suggested that promoting an understanding of individual agency will lead to a greater sense of freedom and creativity for those working within social welfare; of the worth and human potential of the individuals with whom they engage; of the social responsibility of both users, professionals and those who shape services, and of the potential for positive change that agency offers.

ONE

A theoretical introduction

Every person...exercises and has the potential to create some sort of power...The key to understanding power...is...to appreciate how it is expressed, experienced and created by different people at different levels (Fook, 2002, p 53)

Introduction

To make any overall sense to the reader who has no prior acquaintance with the concept of agency, we need first of all to clarify our terms and to explore agency's developing history and why it is believed to have relevance today for social work and social welfare. This first chapter will therefore serve as a theoretical introduction and will fall into three major sections.

The focus of the first section will be on the work of relevant sociological theorists in the evolution of structure and agency theory and on how this process has been influenced by the increasing significance of psychoanalytic insights and, more recently, by post-structural theory, particularly the work of Foucault (Foucault, 1975, 1981). In concluding this section, the writings of Giddens will also be explored (Giddens, 1979, 1991) since not only was it he whose ideas originally inspired this book but also and more importantly, he is generally recognised as the main exponent of structuration theory, which proposes a specific relationship between human agency and social structure. This has been an issue that has constantly preoccupied sociologists. As Margaret Archer rather dramatically described it, 'the fundamental problem of linking human agency and structure stalks through the history of sociological theory' (Archer, 1982, p 455).

In the second section, the major historical and theoretical influences on social work practice during its progress to becoming a distinct area of practice or profession will be explored. In this context, the contributions of Raymond Plant in particular will be drawn out and, more recently, that of Mark Philp, whose ideas, while coming from a differing perspective, effectively complement those of Giddens.

Third, and finally, an attempt will be made to review the relevant literature from the last twenty years, to identify the increasing recognition and influence of agency theory, initially within social policy, but now also within social welfare. It will be suggested that a significant synthesis has recently emerged between sociological and social work theory but that this has not yet been sufficiently recognised and drawn out, an omission that this book will be an initial attempt to address.

Before embarking on this first section, however, we need to clarify some of the terms we will be using.

'Agency', 'systems' and 'structures'

Agency

It is important, in defining the terms we will be using, to stress that they are primarily *concepts*, as opposed to subject areas, approaches or practices (Clark et al, 1990) although an understanding and exploration of them can and arguably should usefully inform our thinking and influence practice. Put simply, 'agency' implies the ability of individuals or groups to act on their situations, to behave as subjects rather than objects in their own lives, to shape their own circumstances and ultimately achieve change. According to Deacon and Mann it means 'actions, activities, decisions and behaviours that represent some measure of meaningful choice' (Deacon and Mann, 1999, p 413).

Barnes (2000) takes this further: 'For an individual to possess agency is for her to possess internal powers and capacities, which through their exercise, make her an active entity *constantly intervening in the course of events ongoing around her*' (p 25, emphasis added). So, in exercising agency, individuals have the potential to influence the events around them and ultimately, in doing so, change the structure of society, which they may perceive as constraining and inhibiting towards them as individuals.

It may be helpful to consider some examples to illustrate what we mean here. On an individual level Diane Blood, in the late 1990s, argued in court to be allowed to use her dead husband's sperm in order to conceive and produce their child. After a protracted legal debate she succeeded and in doing so, laid the ground legally for others to follow in her wake. Similarly, but on a far larger scale, those who took part in the 'poll tax' riots of 1990 or in other forms of resistance to it brought about the abandonment of the tax, and some would argue, to Margaret Thatcher's ultimate downfall later that year. These both represent instances of people exercising agency. In the first example this is on an individual level; in the second, individuals came together to demonstrate collective agency.

Systems and structures

'Systems', conversely, suggest those recurring elements of society that act to sustain it – the combined practices that underpin the effective functioning of our society, with 'structures' referring to the properties of these systems, characterised by the absence of a subject. Systems might be those managed and provided through the state, including, for example, the police force, education and health services and income maintenance and social care. Alternatively, they might consist of more informal institutions such as the family and religious organisations. These are all systems, each of which possesses its own particular structure. For the most part, these entities operate, so to speak, outside and beyond us. We do not question the existence of, for example, the education system, even if we at times take issue about the way in which schools and teachers operate and teach our children. They are simply there, a given, a part of our world as we know and understand it.

These systems have not, however, emerged as if by magic. They are the direct result of individual and collective action, people working together to put in place those structures that are believed to promote the smooth functioning of society. Not only have they been deliberately put in place, they are also maintained and consequently reinforced by individuals, both those working within them and those who use their services.

But this is not to suggest that these systems always operate smoothly and in ways that were originally foreseen. Indeed, unintended consequences can often cast doubt on the efficacy of our institutions. The incidence in hospitals of MRSA, for example, cuts across the idea of them being places of cure and healing; and ongoing debates about the positions occupied in our society by both 'the family' and religion indicate that the form of these institutions too is open to question.

Agency and change

These examples also serve to highlight how these systems and structures are subject to change. If we consider how, for example, the health service operates now, as compared with even fifty years ago, it is clear that there are huge differences, ones that people, acting collectively or in certain instances individually, have brought about. Those suffering from incurable diseases, such as certain forms of cancer, for example, are now given far more information about their condition; and instead of the reality of death being denied and seen as a failure on the part of medical staff, the introduction of hospices, credited to Dame Cicely Saunders, now offer valuable end-of-life care and the opportunity to die with dignity. At a different level, the visiting arrangements for children in hospital have been greatly relaxed and parents are often encouraged to stay in hospital with their children, changes that were brought about, at least in part, by the influential research carried out by James and Joyce Robertson in the 1960s and summarised in *Separation and the very young* (Robertson and Robertson, 1989). How these systems change, how this is conceptualised, and the role individual agents play in this process, are all issues that have bedevilled sociological thinking for over a century and will be the subject for much of this chapter.

This is not, however, to suggest that individual agency is necessarily always a positive force for good or conversely, that structures always operate oppressively, against individual interests, and as it were, 'behind their backs' (Giddens, interpreted by Hoggett, 2001, p 38). Societal systems are indeed vital to the smooth running of our lives; and it could be argued that Hitler was acting very agentically when he presided over the rise of the Third Reich! Rather, the thrust of my argument will be that societal change is brought about by people recognising that things could be otherwise, believing in their own inherent power and acting on their circumstances to achieve positive change.

Agency, moreover, is not to be confused with mere individualism, and 'self-realisation', of the self-centred variety that has characterised much of British society since the 1980s. It is not simply about 'the project of the self', as suggested by Bunting (2004, p 169). Self-awareness and self-actualisation are certainly important aspects of agency, but represent only a part of the whole picture. Of greater significance, certainly in the context of this book, is the mediating role agency takes on in relation to structure and it is this dynamic relationship that we will be considering later in this chapter.

We will now move on to examine the development of relevant sociological theories and how they can inform our thinking about structure and agency today.

Early theoretical perspectives

In the eighteenth and nineteenth centuries, ideas of the individual which emphasised her ability to shape her own destiny lost some of their force under the increasing influence of scientific thought, which gave rise to views which stressed the role of social structures. Since it was these that were seen as of ultimate significance, they became known as 'structuralist' views and highlighted the relationship between society and the individual. Society was seen as something separate and distinct from the individual men, women and children who formed it, as a force which was, as it were, located outside individuals and which operated in such a way as to curb, restrain and ultimately shape their activities. So, for example, forms of religion and patterns of kinship were seen to shape the lives of individuals living in particular societies and in this sense an individual's relationship with society was seen as one where society exercised control over them, a control characterised by some thinkers in negative terms. As Rousseau, the French philosopher, famously described it, 'man is born free, but everywhere he is in chains' (Rousseau, 1762). Individuals, on the other hand, were seen as beings who shared identical qualities. So although there were differences between them such as culture, language and familial patterns, these were seen as superficial; ultimately, in essence, individuals *had* no real individuality, but were reducible to various common, shared characteristics.

Durkheim

This school of thought, known as structuralism, not surprisingly played down, if not completely discounted, the role of individuals as agents. On the contrary, individuals were seen only as able to operate within societal structures or constraints. How society itself changed, adapted and moved on was not addressed adequately, if at all. Emile Durkheim, a French sociologist writing in the second half of the nineteenth century, took this approach further. Representing the functional school of structuralist thought, he promoted the idea of society as a system or organism, where the relationships between its component parts were key. Institutions, groups and individuals all fulfilled a function in sustaining and upholding the state and preserving society, which was seen as of over-arching importance (Durkheim, 1893). Individuals, in Durkheim's analysis, were not seen as sentient people, with unique attributes, but merely as occupiers of roles, roles which had to be filled for society to function effectively. As he wrote, 'Science cannot describe individuals, but only types. If human societies cannot be classified, they must remain inaccessible to scientific description' (Durkheim, 1892). Moreover, those individuals who stepped outside their roles were viewed as deviant, as a threat to society and in need of constraint. Irish and Scottish vagrants, for example, who, in the nineteenth century, came to England during the summer in search of agricultural employment, arguably did not fulfil any useful societal function, and were therefore treated harshly and returned to their countries of origin. Parallels can arguably be drawn today in the way British society responds to and treats asylum-seekers. In Durkheim's analysis people were far from being seen as subjects of their own lives but, on the contrary, as objects, capable of manipulation in the interests of the state, whose needs were paramount.

It is perhaps important to stress here that, while Durkheim's approach arguably over-emphasised the role of the state at the expense of the individual, nevertheless structures and systems are undeniably necessary, for without these society would descend into anarchy and the rule of the most powerful would prevail at the expense of the weakest in society. What Durkheim did not achieve, however, was an account of how these structures could be changed by individuals acting either independently or collectively, as and when the need demanded.

Weber

If Durkheim was a key proponent of the functionalist school, so Max Weber, writing more or less simultaneously, represented the action position within the overall structuralist approach (Weber, referenced in Gerth and Wright Mills, 1948). Weber argued that society consisted of individuals who choose how to act and who are able to construct society according to their own best interests and in this sense, he emphasised agency over structural concerns. Nevertheless, as a sociologist, Weber, like Durkheim, recognised that individuals exist and act within a societal context, and it was this which was of overriding importance.

Hegel, Marx and Engels

Hegel, also writing in the early nineteenth century, moved away from this structurally determined approach, and introduced the idea of 'dialectic', suggesting that, instead of society being a fixed, static entity, it was always progressing. This progress came about gradually through division and discord and through the 'unification of contradictions and opposition' (Plant, 1983, p 190). This way of conceptualising how society changed exerted a strong influence on Marx and his companion and colleague Engels, who, writing in the historically turbulent times of the later nineteenth century, believed that social structures were self-reproducing (Marx and Engels, 1848). They held that just as capitalism had succeeded feudalism, so this in turn would eventually be overthrown by the workers or proletariat, and replaced by a classless structure. This change could be brought about only by revolution and not by gradual, peaceful means. Not only was this change desirable, but according to Marx, it was inevitable and, in analysing change in this manner, he presented a radically different way of conceptualising the relationship between society and the individual. As he described it, 'men make their own history but they do not make it as they please. They do not make it under self-selected circumstances' (Marx, 1852). In this sense, then, Marx was arguably articulating an early and limited definition of agency, limited in the sense of being restricted to revolutionary activity, to the application of force, rather than something that individuals exercise routinely throughout their lives.

Freud

Working and writing around the end of the nineteenth and beginning of the twentieth centuries, Sigmund Freud made a hugely significant contribution to our understanding of human behaviour and motivation (for example Freud, 1900, 1901). He is perhaps best recognised for his interpretation of how the unconscious mind operates and influences our thoughts and actions, and for his description of defence mechanisms, including repression and denial. The importance of Freud's work, and of subsequent psychoanalysts, such as Jung (Jung, 1912, 1921) cannot be overstated, insofar as they have changed our everyday language and our way of understanding ourselves and our fellow human beings. In the present context however, Freud's unique contribution lies in his recognition of the inherent, individual causes of human behaviour, and of the unconscious issues that can influence us throughout our lives. In this sense, Freud was a determinist whose focus was on the individual rather than on society. In his view, the causes of human behaviour were not the result of influences rooted in society, but rather of psychological forces operating within us as individuals, and over which we have little control.

Parsons

Talcott Parsons was one of the first sociologists to recognise the significance of psychological factors and to attempt to reconcile the opposing concepts of structure and agency (Parsons, 1937). Essentially a conservative thinker, Parsons was concerned primarily with society maintaining its equilibrium and in his analysis of behaviour, considered individuals in terms of their membership of different groups or categories, such as the family. He introduced the notion of 'voluntarism' (Parsons, 1937, p 369), by which he implied the voluntary adoption of societal 'norms' by its members, who, in order to further their own ends, chose to internalise these norms and, in doing so, to maintain the social consensus. In addressing the individual actions which flowed from his analysis in this way, Parsons combined societal and psychological factors, a synthesis which he referred to as the 'action frame of reference' (Parsons, 1937, p 733). Within this, however, it was the societal issues that took precedence.

Parsons' analysis faltered, however, when he came to consider *how* society changed and moved on. Since he perceived individual behaviour as dependent on and determined by the system, he had no means of explaining how society could adapt to new circumstances. Indeed, action which did not serve to maintain societal structures was seen as a threat and something which had to be sanctioned and controlled. Moreover, for Parsons, the system was, by implication, upheld by the dominant classes within society, with the 'lower' classes not considered sufficiently intelligent to understand the situation (Parsons, 1937, pp 279-81).

As is probably now clear, neither a structuralist nor an individualist view of society is or can be sufficient, by itself, to explain how society operates. In place of these binary opposites, what is needed is a means of combining the two approaches, a way of conceptualising the ebb and flow of societal relations that allows for and explains the ways in which society changes, adapts and moves on.

Foucault

Writing in the second half of the twentieth century, Michel Foucault was particularly interested in the sources of power and knowledge. His work, associated with the post-structural school, called into question received modernist ideas, based on supposed absolute truths about society (Foucault, 1975, 1981). Instead, the post-structuralists saw knowledge, including knowledge about how society operated, as being fragmented and open to interpretation and change over time and space. In Foucault's view, language and discourse were central to an understanding of power and it was the meanings contained within these that were seen as most significant. 'Discourse', in Foucault's terms, refers to the complex relationship between ideas and things, (Williams, in Parton, 1996, p 64) and to the accepted but constantly-changing truth, at any one time. Since truths and meanings were multiple and inconstant, so power itself was unstable and the sources of power, which in itself was neither 'good' nor 'bad', but neutral, were similarly subject to change.

Crucially, in questioning the fixed, static nature of knowledge, Foucault and his fellow thinkers also challenged the existence of dichotomies and binary opposites. Instead of an either/or approach, where knowledge was either good or bad, right or wrong, they opened up the possibility of different meanings and truths co-existing, of a world where accepting the validity of different opinions and approaches became a possibility. In doing so, they presented a means of including the excluded, of accepting different perspectives as equally valid, and of recognising that power and those who possess it, can be challenged. They understood the possibility, in other words, that those at the bottom of the social ladder were able to exercise power in a similar way to those in positions at the top.

Giddens

Foucault's work was hugely influential and opened up new possibilities for conceptualising how individuals and society interacted. Someone who built on his interpretation of how power operated in society was Anthony Giddens. Better known, perhaps, as the intellectual guru of the early days of New Labour, or as a previous director of the London School of Economics, Giddens' extensive oeuvre nevertheless includes a highly significant contribution to the analysis of structure and agency. His 'structuration theory' introduced a means of conceptualising the mutual dependence of structure and agency, a 'duality of structure', which offered a way out of the existing stalemate (Giddens, 1979).

Giddens argued that neither the theories which emphasise the role of structure at the expense of the individual, nor those which concentrate on individual behaviour or agency are adequate in themselves to explain how society operates. Instead of supporting one or other of these binary positions, he held that structure and agency are mutually dependent, and one cannot exist in the absence of the other. His structuration theory is not rooted in determinism, where too often structure is seen as 'bad' and agency as 'good', but offers a way of conceptualising society that considers both process and outcome, where structure is both enabling and constraining. Structure is not therefore a barrier to action, but is essentially involved in its production through the interaction over time between the two; and institutions do not work, as it were, 'behind the backs' of social actors (Giddens, interpreted by Hoggett, 2001, p 38) since it is these actors themselves who produce and maintain them.

Just as the structure of society shapes individual behaviour, so, over time, individuals themselves influence these structures, which change and develop accordingly. Education departments and schools, for example, in deciding on and delivering the national curriculum, are undoubtedly hugely influential in shaping the learning of children and young people, but have themselves been greatly influenced by particular individuals, such as Jean Piaget, the Swiss philosopher, whose ideas on education psychology had a considerable impact on today's education systems (Piaget, 1928). So, in Giddens' view, the idea is introduced of a dialectical relationship between the individual and society, a relationship where the concepts of time and space are crucially significant. Thus, for example, action itself 'does not refer to a series of discrete acts combined together, but to a continuous flow of conduct' (Giddens, 1979, p 55).

In Giddens' analysis it is not merely the dominant groups who shape the structure of society and whose interests they serve, but the subordinate classes also, who, in deciding not to act to break up these structures, ensure their continuation. Indeed they may, paradoxically, be better served by them than those who appear to be dominant, who may in fact be subject to more limitations on their behaviour.

The royal family, for example, while undeniably extraordinarily wealthy and in historical terms at least, possessing huge political power, are arguably trapped in a way of life where they have no real freedom to travel as and where they want, or to behave in ways that generally would not be seen as compatible with their position. They do, however, fulfil a function that is greatly appreciated by many of their subjects: that of an ongoing real–life soap opera, which serves to amuse, shock and generally entertain society.

In terms of societal norms, it is however, the case that if a large enough number of individuals disobey them, these will be re-negotiated and society will change accordingly. If, for example, the royal family started flagrantly to abuse their position, to behave in ways that the general population deemed beyond the pale, they would cease to be held in the reverence that in some quarters they still are today, and the downfall of the monarchy would no doubt be hastened. Similarly, in recent times, the norm of marriage and the rearing of children within this institution have gradually given way to a situation where stable, non-marital partnerships are seen as having just as much validity and the stigma of illegitimacy has lost most of its currency.

Giddens and power

Like Foucault, Giddens recognised that a key consideration in analysing the relationship between structure and agency is power. Giddens noted that, in the past, this has been viewed as residing predominantly in society, where it has been seen by some commentators to operate as a coercive and negative force over individual agency. Giddens, however, recognising that power in itself is neutral, saw it as also residing in individuals where, in the dialectical relationship between them and society, it has a 'transformative capacity' (Giddens, 1984, p 15). In other words, it is able, over time, to change the structure of society. Power is therefore of crucial significance and since it is vested in both society and individuals, both of which are constantly subject to change, so power relations are themselves always in a state of flux. So too, since it is power existing in individuals which has the capacity to transform, there is always in society the potential for change, arising out of individual agency.

Central to Giddens' theoretical views is the notion that 'things could be otherwise', that societal structures and systems are not immutable and cast in stone, so to speak, but open to influence and change by the individuals that comprise or maintain them. For this to come about, however, individuals need not only to believe in the possibility of change, but, in addition, and most importantly, that they themselves possess the power that can be instrumental in bringing this change about. They need effectively to believe in themselves and in their own transformative potential. Without this self-belief, changes will still happen, but not necessarily ones that are in their own interests.

Giddens does not, however, see individual agency as being, necessarily, associated with intentionality. Instead, he recognises that behaviour can have unintended consequences, based on the implicit power relations involved. So, for example, in our own patriarchal society, where men as a group are collectively more powerful than women, individual men may wish to deny or abrogate this power but find that women still defer to them, because they have been socially conditioned to do so. Alternatively, a social worker, responsible for working with a mother of South-East Asian origin, whose child has disabilities, might decide that the mother would benefit from regular visits to a support group, not realising that this would perhaps be culturally unacceptable to her, and unable to understand why the client is subsequently reluctant to see her, a consequence she was certainly not intending.

In moving away from theories that have tended to see structure and agency as separate and distinct from one another, as, effectively, binary opposites, Giddens has arguably adopted a position which presents a more positive and optimistic view of life. Through acknowledging the dialectical relationship between individuals and society, and the transformative capacity of individual agency, he has developed a theory which is freer, less deterministic and which therefore acknowledges more potential for positive (and negative) change.

Giddens takes his arguments further in *Modernity and self-identity* where he develops the concept of what he refers to as the 'reflexive project of the self', which 'generates programmes of actualisation and mastery' (Giddens, 1991, p 9). He argues that the self is not a passive entity, determined by external influences; but suggests that 'in forging their self-identities...individuals contribute to and directly promote social influences that are global in their consequences and implications' (Giddens, 1991, p 2). They achieve this by continuously revising their 'biographical narratives' through which individuals make sense of their own particular circumstances and in doing so, attempt to combat the sense of personal meaninglessness which he sees as a consequence of the late (or, as others would assert, post-)modern times we live in. Narrative and choice are, according to Giddens, at the very heart of self-identity. We have, he suggests, 'no choice but to choose' (Giddens, 1991, p 81). We shall be returning to many of Giddens' ideas, particularly those relating to power and powerlessness, in Chapter Three, where we will be examining their potential to inform more imaginative and innovative social welfare practices.

Theoretical influences on social work practice

Having briefly looked at the development of some of the more relevant sociological theories, we will now turn our attention to social work theory. In this section, some of social work's main historical and theoretical influences will be outlined and an overview of significant literature attempted. The focus will be on specific periods of social work theory, drawing on the work of key authors who best represent these schools of thought.

The foundations of social work

Social work had its origins in the second half of the nineteenth century. During this period of increasing industrialisation, the gap between rich and poor had widened, and the workless, demoralised poor were perceived by those in better circumstances, as a very real threat, with widespread civil unrest a possibility that had to be controlled and addressed. The poor themselves were not recognised as individuals, but seen as an undifferentiated mass, a mere 'residuum' within society (Stedman-Jones, 1971). Some 'paupers' benefited from charitable gifts, a practice that was thought to be abused, while others only had recourse to the Poor Law and workhouse, run by the local parish, where they were put to doing work, often of a very degrading nature, in return for basic food and lodging. In 1869 the Charity Organisation Society (COS) was founded to investigate the circumstances of individual applicants and assess their suitability for assistance, a practice that was referred to as 'casework'. The COS' approach was essentially a moralistic one, their aim being to distinguish between the 'deserving' and the 'undeserving' poor. According to Woodroofe, this work with individuals not only attempted to address the danger of social revolt, but also to bring out the best attributes in those with whom it worked (Woodroofe, 1962).

By the end of the nineteenth century, a greater understanding of the structural causes of poverty was beginning to emerge. It was gradually realised that the processes of industrialisation resulted in both winners and losers, and that the skills of those who had carried out traditional occupations had often been supplanted by new, more efficient industrial processes. As a result, poverty could not be seen as resulting merely from individual laziness or mendacity but was, at least in part, the consequence of social change. Addressing it therefore came to be seen as a state responsibility, although the 'undeserving', feckless poor were still viewed with suspicion and treated as deviant. According to Philp (1979) social work began to emerge as an occupation at around this time. It occupied the space between the 'respectable' and 'deviant' poor, to work with those who were excluded, and help them realise their social potential. We will return to look more closely at Philp's contribution later on in this chapter.

Social work in the early twentieth century

The seeds of modern social work were sown, however, by the Liberal government of 1906–14. It was this administration that began to introduce, for example, school meals, medical inspections of children in school, health visiting and work with young offenders. From this point onwards, provision for those seen as either deviant or deserving, was no longer to be met simply by philanthropy, but began instead to be seen as the responsibility of the state. The state was not acting simply out of concern for its individual citizens, however, but also from concern about the physical condition of its children, evidenced in those recruited to serve in the Boer War, with the health and hence the efficiency of the future workforce also seen to be an issue. This is a useful instance of how, traditionally, it is when state priorities coincide with those of individuals pressing for reform, as they were doing in the early twentieth century, that change comes about, an example of individual agency interacting with the structures and priorities of the state. Moreover, it is useful to note that in this, as in so many other instances, it was philanthropic action that paved the way for reform and which effectively blazed the trail that the state would ultimately follow.

Although the source of provision had moved from individual philanthropy to the state, the moral imperative behind this Liberal legislation remained the same. The new social services that grew up were still founded primarily on Poor Law notions of morality, and informed by 'knowledge about' rather than 'acquaintance with' those who were at the receiving end of services (James, quoted in Titmuss, 1958, p 19) whose voice was still far from being heard. As Titmuss wrote, 'Classes of persons in need and categories of disease were treated; not families and social groups in distress' (Titmuss, 1958, p 21), and in the subsequent piecemeal approach to social welfare, the primacy of the existing social order remained unchallenged. Indeed, it could be argued that whether to act on the one hand as an agent of the state in upholding state structures and deal simply with 'classes of persons' and 'categories of need', or whether on the other hand to try to work with and understand the individual client has been a perennial dilemma throughout social work's brief history, and one that remains unresolved. It is however an issue that is central to this book and one that we will be attempting to address.

It was in the aftermath of the Second World War and the sweeping social reforms initiated by the Beveridge Report of 1942, referred to as 'the welfare state' that British social work began to evolve into the profession that we recognise today.

In the 1950s and 1960s, social work authors, often writing from a religious viewpoint, tended to highlight the need to acknowledge individuals' inherent dignity, resulting in their possession of certain inalienable, human attributes (Biestek, 1961; Halmos, 1965; Butrym, 1976). Felix Biestek, for example, writing as an ex-priest, argued that all people were 'children of God' and, from this perspective, advocated the adoption of seven casework 'concepts' all of which could be reduced to the overriding principle of 'respect for persons' (Biestek, 1961, p 17). In doing so, he, and others like him (for example Butrym, 1976) were, to this extent, recognising the individuality of those with whom social work engaged and arguably trying to inject a more humane approach into the social work task. What they were advocating, however, did not represent a retreat from a structurally-determined view of human behaviour: they were not effectively challenging the primacy of the state, or its right to prescribe how people should behave and the roles it was their duty, as citizens, to fulfil.

Plant and 'respect for persons'

As Raymond Plant (1970) argued, however, the justification of 'respect for persons' by Biestek and others writing in the same vein, did not go far enough. It did not, for example, necessarily have any validity for atheists, or, in itself clarify how individuals should behave. Rather, it represented merely a pragmatic approach to 'casework': unless individuals were treated with respect, any work with them was unlikely to prove effective. Debatably, in today's social work climate, with its emphasis on efficiency and 'outcomes', this fundamental moral principle and justification for social work intervention, has been eroded in some areas almost to the point of extinction.

Plant, arguably a much over-looked author, takes forward and develops Biestek's concept of 'respect for persons' in ways that have direct relevance to the issues of structure and agency. Focusing, as he was, on the ethical justification for social work, he held that man's moral agency was essentially a transcendental characteristic, one that took precedence over the sum of his role-performances. Hence, part of the central meaning of 'respect for persons' lay in the individual's right to self-direction, a right which flows from the inherent rationality which he argued everyone possesses and which meant that people should not be subject to manipulation, which impeded their rational need to deliberate and choose for themselves. Indeed, he suggested, it was the individual's *responsibility* (emphasis added) to act as the result of his own deliberate thought, rather than passively to react to external circumstances.

The dilemma of social work

Plant went on to assert, however, that much of social work practice denied the reality of client responsibility, with social workers viewing their clients' behaviour as socially deviant, or the result of mental illness.[1] In this way, the behaviour was effectively rendered invalid and the client identified as in need of treatment or social work intervention of some kind. Plant went on to distinguish between negative and positive freedoms, where negative freedom was defined as the right of a client to self-determination, even where the social worker could anticipate that unfortunate consequences for the client might well result from their actions; and positive freedom which resulted from rational self-direction and action. Through knowing and communicating effectively with their client, the social worker would understand that they were not fundamentally committed to those actions associated with negative freedom. It would be the worker's responsibility therefore to exert their professional influence to bring about a more positive outcome.

Plant highlights the primary role of the social worker, as sanctioned by the state, as one of helping individuals adapt to society's norms, and to adjust their behaviour as necessary. Quoting R.D. Laing (1967), however, he asks, 'adaptation to what? To a world gone mad?' (Plant, 1970, p 49). Is it morally right or appropriate to expect an individual to adapt to and accept state repression, for example, or should they rather strive, when appropriate, to bring about societal change? He recognises, however, that because of their social conditioning, individuals cannot easily change their own behaviour or indeed influence societal structures; nor paradoxically, can society itself move on unless the individuals within it do so. In this way, then,

Plant, writing from a social work perspective, questions the determinist stance of social work and effectively identifies the problematic relationship between structure and agency, a theme that was subsequently neglected by social work and which has only recently resurfaced.

Subjective and objective perspectives

Plant's early recognition of this dilemma, his focus on the moral implications of social work practice and his recognition of the social work client as a self-directing agent with the potential to influence society, was soon overtaken and largely over-looked in the work of subsequent theorists, who emphasised different theoretical approaches to social work. If we take the period between the 1960s and 1980, the time at which both Giddens and Philp were writing, the literature was dominated by two main perspectives. The first of these adopted a subjective approach to social work clients. Those adopting this approach argued that the meaning their clients gave to their own situation should take priority and inform any work undertaken with them. Conversely, there were those who took an objective view, who emphasised a more deterministic view of human behaviour. The rest of this section focuses briefly on four main theories within social work, representing these two overarching perspectives: on client-centred approaches, the psychoanalytic school, radical social work and feminist perspectives. The aim will be to demonstrate how these relate to either determinist views of human behaviour on the one hand; or to more individualist interpretations on the other, and we will consider this further later in this chapter.

The client-centred approach

David Howe refers to the client-centred approach to social work, based on humanist psychology, as the 'seekers after meaning', an appropriate description for what they try to achieve (Howe, 1987). The most well-known exponents of this approach include Carl Rogers and George Kelly (Kelly, 1955; Rogers, 1961). Possibly more a philosophy than a specific theory, the Rogerian school of client-centred therapy emphasises the centrality of an empathic, genuine relationship developing between the worker and the client, without which no effective work can take place. The client needs to experience a sense of unconditional acceptance to be able to flourish and move on, something which he has possibly not experienced before and the absence of which is likely to have contributed to his present difficulties. This gap, it is implied, is one that can now partly be filled by the worker, who, for the work to be effective, needs to become emotionally close to the client. Too great a professional distance, it is suggested, militates against a sufficiently close relationship being formed, without which progress cannot be made. Rogerian therapy owes part of its significance to its positive approach to the human condition, not something often associated with social work! It has long been subject to criticism for being arguably too simplistic and 'cosy' in its approach (for example, Clare, 1981); however, what within it has given rise to these objections can perhaps alternatively be construed as both a strength and the source of its appeal.

George Kelly is probably the person most strongly associated with the interactionist school, which alongside Rogerian therapy is the other main client-centred approach. Within this, the practice of labelling clients and their behaviour as perhaps deviant or mentally ill is challenged. Instead, individuals are encouraged, through methods such as personal construct psychology and transactional analysis, to explore the meaning their behaviour has for themselves, turning the professional relationship effectively on its head and taking the view that the client, rather than the worker, is the expert (Kelly, 1955).

An example of the interactionist approach

A teenage offender is asked to interview himself on video, or to write about himself in the third person, as if he were a friend who knew him very well. He is encouraged, in doing so, to describe what goes on inside his head when deciding to commit a particular offence. In adopting this approach, the client assumes the role of subject within their own life, rather than the object of others' interpretations of his behaviour. In achieving this status, he is encouraged to feel a sense of responsibility for his own actions, to recognise that he has a choice as to how he behaves, to move from a position of passivity and helplessness to one where he feels empowered and able to exercise a sense of agency.

Both the Rogerian and the interactionist approaches are ones that have considerable relevance to the main thesis of this book. To quote Howe, 'the ideas people have about what is going on themselves become part of the very social situation in which they are found. That is why it is important to try to understand how the social world looks from the viewpoint of those of whom it consists' (Howe, 1987, p 96). These ideas are ones that we will explore and develop more fully at a later stage.

The psychoanalytic school

In contrast to the 'seekers after meaning', the psychoanalytic school was founded on a scientific approach to individual behaviour, based on the work of Freud and his followers. This gave social work what was seen as a welcome credibility (Jones, 1996) and reinforced its status in the 1960s, as an emerging profession. Its reliance on psychoanalytic insights was, however, only partial, focusing more or less exclusively on individual pathology, and its roots within family dysfunction, while ignoring other Freudian contributions, such as the impact of social structures on individuals (Jones, 1996). Psychoanalytic theory, despite largely falling out of fashion in the 1970s, contributed many insights that are now taken for granted within social work practice, such as an understanding of basic defence mechanisms and of the centrality of dependence within relationships (Howe, 1987). These can help to explain otherwise inexplicable behaviour: why, for example, someone constantly and skilfully changes the subject when it begins to get close to a topic that is too painful for them to discuss; why, when a meeting is about to conclude and there is no time left to talk, a client brings up the issue that is concerning them most; and why, as adults, we both need to depend on others, but often do not allow ourselves to risk such dependence. However, insofar as human behaviour was seen as reducible to early experiences, either positive or negative, the psychoanalytic school has been charged with being overly-determinist and insufficiently open to the possibility of individual change. In this sense, psychoanalytic theory has been criticised for being rather too pessimistic in its orientation.

Radical social work

Radical social work, whose proponents included Bailey and Brake (Bailey and Brake, 1975) and Corrigan and Leonard (Corrigan and Leonard, 1978) emerged in the 1970s, and had its roots in the heady optimism of the previous decade, and in the culture of challenge and protest associated with this. Indeed, this period also gave birth to a number of pressure groups, such as the Child Poverty Action Group and Shelter. In keeping with these movements, radical social work identified structural social problems and particularly adverse socioeconomic circumstances as being the root cause of many of the difficulties faced by their client group. In part, this was also a reaction against social work's overriding focus on individuals and reliance on psychoanalytic insights, which were, by now, increasingly open to question. To put it simply, instead of effectively blaming the client or her family and upbringing for their unfortunate circumstances, society itself was now seen as the villain of the piece. Poverty, in particular, was seen as the result of the failure of capitalist societies, rather than attributable to the shortcomings of individuals and within social work, emphasis was now placed far more on group and community approaches, and on challenging received professional wisdom. Indeed, the whole concept of 'casework', with its associated view of clients as 'culprits' or patients who were in need of 'treatment', came under attack during this period, notoriously, in the 1970s, in the social work magazine *Case Con*, where social work itself was seen as part of the system of oppression. Instead, clients were now characterised as 'victims' of 'the system', and in this way effectively denied any sense of individual responsibility. In moving from a view of human behaviour that was overly determined by issues residing in the individual, social work had now, conversely, adopted a similarly over-simplistic position, in holding society wholly accountable. What was needed was an approach that could encompass both individual and societal factors.

Feminist approaches

Feminist ideas, which attempted to link the personal with the political, went some way towards achieving this goal. Writing in the 1970s and 1980s, feminist theorists (for example, Brook and Davis, 1985; Dominelli and McLeod, 1989) were able to take hold of the insights of the women's movement and develop them in relation to social work. In promoting the value of personal relationships, feminist social work was able to challenge existing practice, and, as was subsequently noted, 'feminist analyses... opened up the possibility of dialogue between professionals and clients, in a participatory approach to the interpretation of need' (Batsleer and Humphreys, 2000, p 10). In validating the uniqueness of individual experience, including that of both the powerful and the powerless, feminists thus discovered a way of acknowledging and incorporating 'the other', and of challenging binary opposition. In other words they gave a voice to those to whom this had previously been denied. Social work practice had, they argued, been based until now on male-dominated views of what was acceptable behaviour in women, in wives, mothers and daughters. By labelling some mothers as 'inadequate', when, for example, they did not keep the house clean or their children were seen as undernourished and thin, men were reducing their behaviour to what they, acting as society's self-appointed representatives, felt was appropriate, even though this denied the lived experience of many of those thus categorised, whose behaviour might in fact be a rational response to their circumstances. In this sense, female social work clients were once again cast effectively in the role of victims. However, by recognising this and by bringing women's personal experience of their situations out into the open it was believed that the inherent imbalance in gender relations and the associated oppression practiced by men towards women could be unmasked and confronted. Women, both social workers and clients, were encouraged to find a voice, to act collectively and in cooperation with each other, in an attempt to turn received ideas on their heads and challenge the status quo. So, in the early 1970s, for example, the Women's Aid movement was developed in recognition of the domestic violence suffered by women behind closed doors. This was an attempt not only to bring the reality of abuse out into the open, and to validate women's experiences and offer support, but also, importantly, to challenge the patriarchal system and the way women's behaviour was perceived.

At this point, however, feminist social work theory was challenged, not from outside, but from within its own ranks. Lynne Segal (Segal, 1987, cited by Hudson in Langan and Lee, 1989) highlights that particular groups of women began to argue that feminism itself was oppressive, in marginalising those who were outside the mainstream, for example, lesbian women, those with disabilities and women from minority ethnic groups. In this way, feminism effectively started to fragment internally, as more emphasis was placed on the issues that divided women, rather than on what could unite them. Not only were there differences between different groups of women, but their interests were potentially at odds with each other, with white, heterosexual, middle-class, able-bodied women able to exercise power over those who were outside this group. Having earlier put the case for individuality and inclusivity, so feminism, ironically, was now itself pushed into a position of adopting 'either/or' positions.

These divisions seriously weakened the feminist argument, and its belief in itself was shaken. However, from a postmodern perspective, this same fragmentation of opinion was very much part of the prevailing zeitgeist and, as we will identify, helped to lay the foundations for a new way of conceptualising social work, to re-define what its purpose is and how it can and arguably should be practised.

The client in society

Reviewing these theoretical positions then, and at risk of considerable over-simplification, we can see that, in their different ways, each was pushing forward an understanding of the client's position in society. Each represented some advance, but no one position provided an adequate explanation for how, using the experiences and insights from those with whom social work uniquely engages, society as a whole could learn, adapt and move on. The client-centred approach lays great emphasis on the centrality and validity of the client's own perspective and the need for the worker to engage closely with and learn from them but, as the name implies, does not move on to consider how this understanding can then influence wider society. The psychoanalytic school focuses on addressing individual emotional and behavioural problems, which it sees as rooted in the client and in her life history, but does not take sufficient account of her societal existence. However, its contribution, in putting forward, for the first time, the idea of subconscious motivation for behaviour is highly significant. Radical social work, in focusing on the faults of 'the system' and casting clients in the role of victims, tends to deny their own responsibility for their situation and the power they possess, as individuals, to change their circumstances. Nevertheless, both in its talk of class struggle and resistance and in its giving rise to later democratic models of user-involvement (Pearson, 1975, referenced in Ferguson, 2008) the radical school was implicitly laying the ground for a consideration of the role of individual and group agency in social work practice. Finally, the feminist school not only seeks to validate the particular experience of women, both as individuals and as a group; it also goes some way to demonstrate how an understanding of their circumstances, and those of other oppressed groups, lying outside the mainstream, can influence the way society itself is structured.

What was still arguably needed, however, was a way in which positive change, at both an individual and a societal level, could be theorised. This was needed all the more since the very act of believing in the possibility of change contains within it the potential of injecting more hope and optimism into the social work task, something which in itself would represent welcome progress within the profession.

The contribution of Philp

Just as Giddens represented a watershed in sociological thinking, so the work of Mark Philp demonstrates a significant leap forward within social work theory. Published interestingly in the *Sociological Review*, rather than in the social work press, Philp's article was an attempt to 'grasp social work theoretically' (Philp, 1979, p 85). In doing so, he focused on the 'form of knowledge' in social work which he argued needed to be subjectless, or in other words, existing above and beyond any particular individual perspective. He criticised the thinking of Pearson and others from the radical school for believing that their own views could be objective and for not recognising and questioning their own values and beliefs. He argued that social work knowledge needed to get underneath, so to speak, these and other theories and in attempting to achieve this, he drew from other theoretical areas, such as sociology, social policy and philosophy. Like Giddens, Philp was writing at the end of the 1970s, itself a political turning point in recent history and he drew on the work of Foucault and other post-structural theorists, using discourse theory to illuminate his own ideas. Discourses, as he explained, act as linkages between different statements and operate 'within the same regimes of truth' (Philp, 1979, p 87). So in social work, the prevailing discourse is concerned with the ways in which we view and conceptualise those groups with whom we work, whether they be young offenders, vulnerable older people or drug-users, for example, and is itself influenced by the particular political and cultural context in which it operates.

Social work and the knowledge associated with it arose, according to Philp, in the space that emerged in the nineteenth century between the two discourses of the rich on the one hand and the poor on the other, or, as described by Parton (Parton, 2008, drawing from Pearson, 1975 and Jones, 1983) between the respectable and the dangerous classes, those with political influence and those who were socially excluded. In operating at this social juncture, it attempted to demonstrate the humanity of the privileged to the poor and the essential 'goodness' of the poor to the privileged (Philp, 1979, p 96). This space provided the 'conditions of possibility' (Foucault, quoted in Philp, 1979, p 88) for the new discourse of social work to emerge. This was the period when, as we have already indicated, those in possession of wealth and power came, more and more, to fear the increasingly powerful voice of the poor and dispossessed and the threat of social revolt. In these circumstances, social work was required to act as both 'social sedative and regulator' (Woodroofe, 1962, p 50, cited in Philp, 1979, p 94) and to try 'to bring the poor back to be self-respecting members of society' (Woodroofe, 1962, p 51, cited in Philp, 1979, p 94). Social work then, was operating in a 'dual role', something that has remained a constant factor throughout its history and which has been a perennial source of unease for social work professionals ever since.

Philp's unique theoretical contribution lies both in his understanding and his account of the paradox at the heart of social work. This paradox had been recognised but not fully explored by others before him. Pearson, for example, spoke of the 'delicate fabric of this interface between the *individual* and *society*' and recognised that 'social welfare exists on the hinge of this paradox' (Pearson, 1975, in Jones, 1975, p 54). What Philp went on to clarify, however, was that, while trying to achieve objectivity about those with whom it works – drawing for example on sociological or psychological knowledge – social work is in fact always discussing subjects, unique individuals, those who are, as he describes it 'characterised by a universal subjectivity, one which applies to all individuals and yet to no-one in particular' (Philp, 1979, p 91). Whilst other disciplines are able to draw on objective knowledge in describing the shared characteristics of, for example, 'the poor' or 'single parents', the role of social work is to attempt to return to subjective status those who are not currently viewed by society as subjects but rather as objects; those who today, are often referred to as the 'socially excluded'. So social work 'negotiates on behalf of the mad, the bad and the stigmatised; between those who have been excluded from power and those who have the power to exclude...between the sound in body...and the handicapped, between the law abiding and the law breaking...and the sane and the borderline' (Philp, 1979, p 97), attempting to bring them back into acceptability. In doing so, social work's task must be to identify the underlying worth of the individuals with whom they engage, to recognise the good in their clients and represent their potential as future social beings (Philp, 1979).

It is perhaps helpful here to consider how, in our practice today, we can choose to emphasise either the external and structural or the individual and psychological determinants of human behaviour. Philp offers the useful example of writing social enquiry reports, known today as 'pre-sentence reports', for offenders facing sentencing. He describes how the authors of these reports, depending on the outcome they are trying to achieve for their client, may stress, on the one hand, the structural influences bearing down on them – the poverty they suffer, their worklessness, or their lack of formal education. In this way, they will be presenting a view of their client as a passive victim of circumstance, unable or struggling to act on their own account, but instead driven to offend by forces that are effectively beyond their control (Philp, 1979, p 98). Put differently, they are adopting a structurally determined view of their client, seeing his behaviour as determined by forces external to him rather than the outcome of personal decisions he himself has made. Wanting to create a different impression however, the author of the report may, alternatively, emphasise the individual's own choice in relation to their behaviour, the fact that this is a less serious offence than their former ones and that, in the context of this particular offender, it represents an improvement. In this way, the client is being presented as an active subject, someone who has an internal, personal existence, who can reflect on his actions and make choices about how he behaves and lives his life. We will be exploring these distinctions more fully at a later stage.

Philp's analysis is rooted in a moral concern for social work clients, and in this sense he echoes those theorists of the mid-twentieth century to whom we have already referred, particularly Biestek (1961), Halmos (1965, cited on p 16) and Plant (1970). However, he also argues that 'social work knowledge describes a process where... individual states and objective statuses are transformed into a social subject: *marked by capacities for self-determination, responsible citizenship and general sociability'* (emphasis added) (Philp, 1979, p 92). In this sense, his contribution is allied not only to Plant, but arguably perhaps has echoes of Giddens, and his account of the 'transformative capacity' of individual agency.

In summary then, Philp's important contribution for the purposes of this book is his combined focus both on the essentially moral nature of social work intervention, and the optimism associated with his recognition of the potential for social work clients to return or be returned to subjective status, to become, in other words, active agents in their own lives. Alongside Giddens' insights, it is these twin elements that contribute to an understanding of the role and potential of individual agency which we will be exploring throughout the following chapters.

Recent developments in social work theory and practice

Finally in this chapter, we will move on to explore the ways in which the ideas of both Giddens on the one hand and Philp on the other have influenced theorists in the last 30 years. It is significant that, during this period, especially over the last ten years, there has been a growth of interest in agency, in both how it is conceptualised and what it has to offer, particularly in the field of social policy. In this last section, therefore, we will consider and assess the contribution of some of these authors, who have written from both sociological, social policy and social work perspectives, and identify where these cross over and meet each other in between. I will conclude by attempting to synthesise what these writings have to offer in terms of social work practice.

The recognition of agency

The new focus in the literature of the 1980s and 1990s on individual experience and identity both contributed to and flowed from postmodern theory on the one hand and feminist ideas on the other, each of which, in turn, arguably helped to shape the other. Together with the considerable influence of Giddens' writings, this led, for the first time, to a consideration in the literature of subjectivity and the notion of agency. As Kirk Mann, writing in 1985 put it, until now the subjects of social policy had only entered the stage as 'social problems' and, quoting Charles Dickens, 'what they are unto themselves remains a mystery' (quoted in Mann, p 65). Earlier analyses of the welfare state, he held, had over-emphasised structural issues and in doing so had reinforced a sense of powerlessness within welfare recipients. As he put it, 'In order to explain how men and women make history in particular circumstances we need an account sensitive enough to disentangle human agency from structural effect' (Mann, 1985, p 72). Instead of being recognised as potential agents for change, however, the poor had, until now, merely been defined by their lack of agency (Deacon and Mann, 1999).

Williams et al, (1999) considered the effect on social work theory of the fragmenting of overriding ideas about how society works, one of the consequences of postmodernism. They recognised the opportunity this provided for connecting sociological insights with those from a psychological perspective, focusing instead on the need for empowerment. They distinguished between the old paradigm, put forward by radical social workers, that emphasised structural inequalities, and the more recent emphasis on stress and coping which they argued had become outdated. They held that what was needed now was an account that simultaneously took into consideration psychological, sociological and social policy influences. Indeed, it has been suggested elsewhere (Williams, 1999; Barnes, 2000) that the concept of agency came into being partly as a reaction against over-determinist views of human behaviour, with individuals merely responding to external events, and seen simply as passive recipients of services and members of fixed categories, such as 'the poor'; or, as Williams et al (1999) would also argue, determined by and responding to their individual circumstances, their personal background and internal psychological pressures. The political concept of social exclusion which arose in the 1980s, moreover, reinforced this view of people being denied a sense of individuality or agency. It is its potential to synthesise these hitherto opposing views of individual behaviour that arguably distinguishes agency theory from its predecessors and lends it its force, something to which we will return in the Conclusion.

The focus on experience and identity

In the 1980s, a new focus emerged in the literature on experience and identity, on the actual lives of social work clients, and how these lives were experienced by them as individuals. This represented a move away from the over-arching views and theories associated with modernism with its emphasis on scientific methods of assessment and measurement, and where the state was seen as strong and coherent (Parton and O'Byrne, 2000). It marked instead the beginning of a recognition of what postmodern and post-structural thinking had to offer social work. Writing from a research perspective, Williams et al (1999) stressed, for example, the need to move on from scientific quantitative analysis to a greater emphasis of qualitative methods, ones that recognised the 'research subject as a creative human agent' (p 41). They acknowledged, however, the continuing need to remain aware of structural constraints on individuals and believed that social work was uniquely placed to synthesise the insights from both structure and agency frameworks in its practice. They also stated, however, that social work was not currently competent in this regard. As they noted 'the relationships between notions of identity, subjectivity, agency and socio-economic circumstances remain largely untheorised' (Williams et al, 1999, p 159). Moreover, to the extent that the importance of validating the lives of clients was recognised, this was restricted largely to theory and the direct practice of social work. The views of policy makers and managers, conversely, tended to remain locked into modernist ideas and approaches. We will return to this in the final chapter.

Citizenship

The potential for a consideration of agency being more adequate in addressing the lives of poor people, and better placed to reflect difference and diversity was welcomed by various authors. Ruth Lister (in Barry and Hallett, 1998, p 37) recognised, in her exploration of citizenship, that citizens were seen now less as 'passive bearers of rights' and more as active political agents; while Deacon and Mann (1999) lamented the fact that 'the poor...have rarely featured as active agents of change' (p 415) but noted that post-structural thinking had now allowed for the poor to have a voice 'albeit one that was off stage heckling' (p 419). They also recognised that this voice was resisted in some social policy quarters through fears both that acknowledging diversity would lead to the fragmentation of social policy and that offering meaningful choice to the poor would result in 'wrong' choices being made, resulting in greater expenditure on welfare to 'bail out' individuals. They conclude, however, by stating that:

> Welfare policy is either about enabling people to make responsible choices or it is a form of social engineering. If it is the former, then it must engage with behaviour and the moral decisions that people make. If it is the latter, then the debate is about what sort of society it wants to engineer and which set of moral codes it wishes to impose. The tension between these options cannot be resolved; policy will either treat the poor as moral defectives or as moral agents. (Deacon and Mann, 1999, p 433)

The notion of agency was welcomed from other perspectives too. The psychoanalyst, Susie Orbach, referred to 'the elusive and yet crucial concept of personal agency, of subjectivity which needs to be more centrally addressed in social policy initiatives' (Orbach, 1999, p 13). She saw a consideration of agency as having the potential to bring together the various aspects and concerns of psychoanalysis: of hearing and bearing witness to its clients; of valuing their experience; of understanding their emotional states and how these can change between, for example, sadness and anger in the absence of a sense of acceptance; of the feelings associated with social exclusion; and of the inherent meaning of individual behaviour, especially where this is otherwise construed as destructive.

The self as reflexive project

The idea of agency as rational action is linked to Giddens' original notion of the self as a reflexive project (Giddens, 1991). Reflexivity presupposes the ability of individuals to move beyond passivity and instead to exercise resourcefulness, and their ability to 'critically reflect on their actions...in ways that may reconstitute how...they...act and feel and even reshape the very nature of self identity itself' (Ferguson, 2003, p 199). Drawing on Giddens and the work of Ulrich Beck (Beck, 1993), Ferguson argues that, as science and religion have lost much of their authority, there are now 'new opportunities for ordinary citizens to be reflexive and knowledgeable about society and themselves exercise choices about how to live, as well as new obligations to shape their lives' (Ferguson, 2003, p 201). In doing so, they are able to demonstrate how they can turn constraints into opportunities and can contribute, as active citizens, to emerging welfare practices. Moreover, implicit in the changing nature of self-awareness is the sense that reflexivity is a process, not a fixed state of affairs. It is therefore concerned with change, change that is accomplished over time and space.

The sense of the self as a reflexive project existing over time is taken further by Hoggett (2001). He introduces the idea of internal conflict and the existence of a number of different selves, which the individual has to choose between. Quoting Craib (1992, p 172) Hoggett (2001) points out that 'we might feel that one part of ourselves has decided something and that another part is fighting against it' (p 41). In recognising this inner conflict, which may well take place at an unconscious level, Hoggett acknowledges the significance of the Freudian concept of denial, and how this can account for our inability on occasion to explain why we act as we do, why we make particular decisions and choices and why we sometimes act as our own worst enemy. He describes this type of involuntary action, where we act against our better judgement, as non-reflexive, non-rational action, but action that is nevertheless committed by individuals acting as agents. This model of agency is, he argues, 'much more able to handle paradox and contradiction' (Hoggett, 2001, p 53), particularly useful, it is suggested, in considering agency in relation to social work, where these issues are often central. It also, as Hoggett points out, allows for the existence, even in a client who is severely depressed, or, perhaps, very resistant to social work intervention, of there being another aspect of them with which we can connect, which can form the basis of a therapeutic alliance. It allows, in sum, for the reality that identity is in a constant state of change (Fook 2002). This is a very important consideration and one to which we will return in subsequent chapters.

Limitations of the binary approach

The inadequacy of theories committed to one or other binary opposed positions, to 'either/or' arguments, was touched on earlier in this chapter. Social work, for example, has often been cast in the role either as agent of enforcement and state control, or as a source of care and empowerment, although practitioners will be very aware that both aspects are and indeed often need to be centrally involved. As Pearson put it, 'Social work has the dual obligation to man *and* society' (Pearson, in Jones, 1975, p 55). In this context, the contribution of feminist social work theory in beginning to move these boundaries, and in recognising the validity of all individual experience, of 'both/and' was recognised. Theories about the individual and society and the relationship between them have similarly tended to approach their analysis from either a structure or an agency perspective, blaming either society or the individual for social ills.

In terms of power dynamics, this binary approach has resulted in those at the margins, the potential client group of social welfare whose existence is characterised by their relative powerlessness, being pushed further out of sight, to a point where their needs are ignored by the powerful (Lukes, 1974, quoted in Mann, 1985; Fook, 2002). It has, in other words, contributed to the process of marginalisation. Too great an emphasis, for example, on what are accepted by society as 'normal' and acceptable behaviours, can only, arguably, result in increased levels of intolerance towards those whose behaviour lies outside these narrow definitions; and to their consequent social exclusion. What has been needed but until now been notably absent has been a way of theorising that includes both issues of time and space and a way of conceptualising power, that explains how individuals, even those at the margins, can and do change society, a way of understanding individual actors or agents themselves, 'an account sensitive enough to disentangle human agency from structural effect' (Mann, 1985, p 72). What is now emerging, however, from the new theorising about agency, initiated by Giddens' ideas on structuration, is this very recognition of the dynamic interplay between structure and agency, of agency's transformative potential, and of how each affects and has an impact on the other. This has resulted in a realisation of agency's potential to synthesise differing viewpoints, which again has been welcomed by a number of authors. As Jencks has argued, for example, 'we need to replace our instinctive either/or approach to blame with a both/and approach' (Jencks, 1994, quoted in Deacon and Mann, 1999, p 432).

Finally, there is the important issue of how those whom we encounter as social welfare recipients or as social work clients, actually view themselves and their own behaviour. There is considerable evidence that, unlike many of those who work with them, social work clients do not usually cast themselves in the role of victim, or, even when living below the breadline, necessarily see themselves as poor. On the contrary, many people take pride in 'getting by' and 'making do' and in doing so, resist the labels that others are inclined to place on them. They see themselves, in other words, as 'us' not 'them', as active agents in their own lives, rather than people simply affected passively by their external circumstances (Deacon and Mann, 1999). Indeed, this evaluation of them and their lives is more often, arguably, the result of the 'lamentable arrogance of social casework' (Deacon and Mann, 1999, p 417). Titterton in contrast, refers to 'the differentiated nature of vulnerability and risk among individuals and the role of creative human agency in responding differentially to well-being across the lifespan' (Titterton, 1992, p 2, cited in Williams et al, 1999, p 9). This potential of human agency is an area that we will explore in greater detail in Chapter Two.

Conclusion

To summarise this first chapter, we will now attempt to synthesise and bring together the ideas expressed by these authors, what they tell us about the potential for human agency, and why this is arguably so significant in a consideration of social work and broader social welfare.

First, an understanding of agency offers us a new way of conceptualising the individual and her relationship to society. It offers a means of recognising that the conditions that shape her existence should not be seen as inevitable, as in themselves wholly deterministic of her life and circumstances, but are themselves the results of individual behaviour and decision making and therefore susceptible to change. They can, consequently, be related to in a different way, seen not just as constraints on behaviour but as conditions within and upon which individuals can exercise their own agency; can, indeed, seek to bring about change (Beck, 1993). This, in itself, can hopefully begin to lay the ground for a more constructive, optimistic approach to social work and welfare.

Second, a consideration of agency provides a possible means of countering the current preoccupation within social welfare of targets, outcomes and competencies, which in their emphasis on scientific measurement, fail to honour and recognise the variety, richness and diversity of human experience, and perhaps, what is most important, to measure both what individuals view as a high priority in their lives and the resources they themselves can bring to bear in addressing their circumstances. Instead, the concept of agency illuminates the need for service planners to be in continuing dialogue with clients and with individual professionals, an issue that was raised as far back as 1970 (Mayer and Timms, 1970) but rarely been given the prominence it deserves since.

Further, simply placing the lives and experiences of service users centre-stage, as it were, and considering them as the subjects of their own lives rather than the objects of policy and social work intervention, can change our perspective. This very act of validating their experience, of putting this first, provides a means of empowering otherwise marginal people, of legitimating their unique experiences and identities and focusing on them as individuals. Indeed, Titterton has implied that the very practice of referring to 'unmarried mothers' or 'the elderly' in an undifferentiated way contributes to these people being viewed as a potential social problem, as unlike 'us', but as 'the other'. It is therefore part of the cause of their social exclusion. Fook claims, furthermore, that postmodern theory in itself challenges the very idea of professional expertise, with the views of ordinary citizens being granted relatively greater status and recognition (Fook, 2002). So an awareness of agency and a conscious adoption of practices by social work practitioners that can be recognised as agency-enhancing, can lead to a new form of empowerment, one that not only gives clients, *qua* clients, a greater voice, but also assists them to move beyond this role, to become self-directing actors or agents in their own lives – and to influence their own and others' circumstances. In other words, and most important, it offers a new way of focusing on clients as 'active agents in shaping their lives, experiencing, acting upon and reconstituting the outcomes of social policies' (Williams et al, 1999, p 2).

In Chapters Two and Three, we will be considering the concept of agency specifically in relation to the social work task, to examine how it can help illuminate and inform the most productive forms of practice. In doing so, we need to move on from the idea merely of social workers acting for and on behalf of their clients, to a perspective that increasingly takes into account what clients can do for themselves, a view which, moreover, takes us beyond the involvement of the worker to the point where the client is restored to subject status within their own life (Philp, 1979) is acting on their own behalf and, in doing so, is expressing their own agency.

In these next chapters we will therefore be exploring ideas, based not on a pathological view of those with whom we work, but on one that emphasises a more constructive, optimistic approach: that draws on notions of resilience, adaptability, resourcefulness and a personal 'sense of coherence' (Antonovsky, 1979); and that considers the centrality of 'relationship' to social work, not just that between the worker and their client, but also that between the client and their external world. We will also be taking into account the crucial nature, as Giddens recognised, of self-belief, the idea that 'things could be otherwise' and how these beliefs in themselves can bring about positive change. In doing so, we will be considering how circumstances and relationships change over time, how the client can change from the objectified focus of societal concern to being the self-directing subject of their own lives; and what is most important, how she can bring about change, individually and alongside others, in wider society and in doing so, help to influence those very structures that shape her own life.

Note

[1] The people with whom social workers engage were referred to until the late 1980s as 'clients'. It was soon after the Griffiths Report of 1988 that they became known as service users. In this chapter, which deals largely with historical texts and accounts of social work, I shall therefore make consistent use of this term to avoid confusion, but will refer to them as 'service users' in subsequent chapters.

TWO

Social workers and service users

The identification and amplification of personal agency is central to
constructive social work. (Parton and O'Byrne, 2000, p 60)

Introduction

In the first chapter, we introduced the concept of agency, and examined its
relationship to structure. We considered definitions and noted how structure and
agency theory was developed within the field of sociology. We went on to consider
the emergence of social work and the context within which it has operated over
the last 150 years; and identified how the literature relating to social work and social
policy has shared some of the same concerns over the last thirty years. Finally, we
began to consider the relevance and potential of individual agency for the field
of social care and how various authors have begun, increasingly, to identify this
in the social work literature. We concluded by recognising that an understanding
of agency can be helpful in informing both our own practice as social workers,
and can also enable service-users to gain more control over their own lives – and
in doing so, help change the very context within which they – and we – live.

In this chapter, it will be suggested that an appreciation of agency theory by those
involved in social care, and an understanding that individual agency is central in
achieving change, is fundamental to the profession. Some methods and approaches
that may serve to enhance the agency of service users and ultimately influence
what they can achieve will be explored. Key concepts that we will consider include
the transformative capacity of individual agency, and the centrality of belief both
in oneself and in the possibility of change. We will also examine the notions of
rational choice, intentionality and unintended consequences and begin to explore
the notion of power as exercised by both social workers and service users.

The significance of the social worker

It may be stating the obvious, but who a social worker is, what their philosophical
beliefs are, what their value base is, and how this informs their practice, are crucial
to the experience of the service user. The need for a value base is, of course, also
endorsed by the General Social Care Council and by professional organisations
such as the British Association of Social Workers. What social workers consider
as the fundamental purpose of their work, how they perceive service users and
their potential, whether they believe that change is possible, or even desirable – all
these factors exercise a significant influence on the way they carry out their work.

Social work approaches: two examples

Worker 'A' is very efficient and enthusiastic, good at time-keeping and getting through her work and more willing than most to take on extra cases at referral meetings. The approach she adopts is, for obvious reasons, positively rewarded by her manager, particularly because she is well liked and no complaints are ever received about her work. It may not be noticed that it is the service users with whom she engages who are more likely to be re-referred, who remain 'stuck' in certain behaviour patterns, and who start to resist subsequent involvement with both social work and other professionals.

Worker 'B' takes more time with his clients, thinks more carefully about how to approach his work with them and which methods are most appropriate, and is less prepared to pick up new cases from his manager. He is also more obviously concerned about his service-users' progress and what will happen to them once his relationship with them ceases. This behaviour is less positively rewarded by management: indeed, the worker concerned is seen as over-involved with his clients and perceived as a nuisance within the team. It may be, however, that the users involved with the second worker are better pleased with the service they receive, retain or regain their self-respect and ultimately achieve more lasting change.

So what happens to social workers and their commitment to their work once they are qualified? It is to be hoped that most people come into the profession feeling enthusiastic and with a firm belief in the worth of individual service users, of their potential to achieve positive change, and of their own transformative ability to help bring that change about; and some workers are fortunately able to sustain this commitment and value base throughout their career. Such, however, are the stresses and strains of the work and the high case-loads that, after a certain length of time, as a recent survey has shown, there are others who start to lose their original enthusiasm and ideals (Mickel, 2009).

Social worker attitudes

Social workers tend to divide into one of two groups. For some, they start to suffer from 'compassion fatigue', gradually losing the sense that each of their clients is unique, and becoming tired not only of their work, but also of the clients themselves (Roche, 2003). For this group, the work tends to become simply routine. They carry out the required assessments on parents, young people, or sick or vulnerable older people more or less adequately, write up their recording and reports promptly or otherwise, and complain about their workloads. For them, the work has generally ceased to be stimulating and interesting; one case is much like another, varying only in details or emphasis. They can't wait to get to the end of the day, the weekend, or even their working life. The work is, in effect, just another job, where service users are categorised, visited and assessed, targets are met or fail to be reached – and any original sense of true engagement with unique individuals is lost, along with any optimism or belief in their capacity to change. Instead, clients are seen very much as society so often portrays them, as the authors of their own misfortune, as failures and outcasts, and as people who are essentially unlike ourselves, as 'the other'.

For the second group, it is 'the system' that they feel is rotten and at fault. These workers probably sympathise and identify with service-users, but in merely acting out their prescribed role as servants of the state, feel as powerless as them in their inability to change anything. This group perceive the state and its structures to be ultimately to blame for their own and society's ills. They are, to use Garfinkel's term, 'cultural dopes' (Garfinkel, 1967). They are not themselves able to make individual choices, still less to influence events, or so they believe. Along with their clients, they view themselves as victims, unable to have an impact on policies and procedures that bear down on them and those with whom they work. They have a sense of inevitability and hopelessness that not only leaves them frustrated, but which also pervades the work itself, renders them passive, and communicates itself inevitably to service users. Unless social change comes about that ameliorates the effects of poverty and discrimination, no useful change can, in their view, come about. On the contrary, all that social workers have to offer amounts to no more than a sticking plaster over the weeping sore of social oppression.

So what is actually happening to these two groups of social workers, why does it happen so often and is there anything that can be done about it? It is, of course, not surprising that the type of work in which we engage, the physical conditions and emotional pain experienced by so many service users and the associated degree of suffering we encounter, not to mention the degree of adverse media publicity that we so often have to contend with, will leave many of us struggling and feeling 'burned out' and exhausted. Under these circumstances, it is perhaps inevitable that we will resort to defensive behaviour of one sort or another. What is interesting, however, is the determinist nature of both of the two characteristic defensive positions described. With the first group, it is the individual service user who is overly determined and who is objectified and denied a sense of individuality and worth. In the second instance, it is society that is held to blame, and seen as wholly accountable for the conditions that service users endure, and that we, as those who work with them, have also to contend with. In both cases, we fail to recognise that things could be otherwise, that any given set of circumstances is open to change, and that both service users and we ourselves possess transformative potential. We fail, in other words, to believe in our own and others' personal agency. In doing so we deprive ourselves and those with whom we work of hope, of a belief that things can and do change, and the knowledge that we can act to help bring this about.

Social work, agency and structural oppression

It is important to recognise, however, the relationship between individual agency and structural oppression. As social workers, we need to retain a focus not just on the individual, but also on society and societal factors, to recognise what, within their lives, is the responsibility of the service user and what is beyond their control, and the result, instead, of structural issues. Focusing exclusively on the potential of service users to exercise their own agency to resolve their problems is to recognise only half of the situation. As professionals, we need to remain aware of the possible structural causes of their difficulties, and, where possible, use our own agency to help bring about change.

Another example of professional practice

As a family support worker, working in a voluntary agency, you have recently started work with a young asylum-seeking, single mother from Ethiopia. She has recently moved with her three young children into privately rented accommodation, in a deprived area of a large industrial city. The family's living conditions are cramped, there is no garden and the house opens straight onto a busy road, where the traffic accident rate is high. The nearest park is 15 minutes walk away. The mother, Sadie, has been referred by her GP, who has been treating her for depression and is concerned for the safety and well-being of her children. Sadie has no friends or relatives in the city and has fallen out with her neighbours, who have complained about the noise her children make. On your initial visit, Sadie is slow to engage with you, avoids eye contact, and talks only to the children, who seem to relate well to her.

Using your professional skills, you encourage Sadie to talk and gradually build up a picture of her life. She has fled, with her children, from Ethiopia, where she has witnessed prolonged violence and her husband has been killed. As a hospital administrator in her home country, she is a woman of considerable intelligence and resourcefulness and has managed to get herself and her children to England where she thought she would be able to find work and reasonable accommodation. In reality, she is not legally able to work and her accommodation and general circumstances, together with her experiences over the recent past, have left her demoralised and depressed. She knows no-one and feels persecuted by her neighbour, with whom she had hoped to become friendly. Instead, this woman seems prejudiced against her as an asylum-seeker, who, in her view, is 'living off the state and should go back where she came from'.

Sadie is clearly someone who has, in the past, believed firmly in her own agency and ability to act on her circumstances. It is, after all, this self-belief that has enabled her to come to England with her children and find accommodation. After what she has recently endured, however, this faith in herself has now, not surprisingly, been dented, and she is exhausted and disillusioned by the reality of life in England. As her worker, you feel empathy for Sadie and the in which situation she finds herself, and, once she starts to trust you and to realise that you are there to help her, she clearly appreciates and benefits from being able to talk freely to you about her feelings. However, you realise that, for things to improve, Sadie has to be encouraged and enabled to take on what responsibility she can for her own life and for moving things forward herself. You therefore put her in touch with a local agency that supports asylum-seekers, and arrange for them to make an initial visit to her. They will be able to advise her on her legal rights and ensure that she is receiving all the benefits to which she and her children are entitled. You also encourage her, along with her children, to attend the local Sure Start Children's Centre, where you know that, in the mixed community where Sadie now lives, there are other parents in similar situations to her own and where she is likely to make friends and feel less alone. There are also staff there who will recognise Sadie's abilities and potential and encourage her not only to join in with existing provision, but also, when she is ready, to contribute to activities and share her own ideas and experience for the benefit of others. In encouraging Sadie in this way, she will hopefully come to realise that she is still capable of dealing with some of her own problems, and in doing so will be energised and move out of her depression. She may even, eventually, be able to offer support to others in her own situation.

This is not the end of the story, however, and as her worker you arguably have further responsibilities towards Sadie. Using your own sense of professional agency, it is important that you challenge the external constraints she has been facing. Believing that the quality of housing she has been offered is unacceptable, and with Sadie's knowledge and permission, you contact the local organisation supporting asylum-seekers, using their expertise to improve your understanding, if necessary, of their circumstances, and discuss with them how the situation might be improved locally for asylum-seekers in future. You may also decide to find out, through local professional networks, how widespread are the sort of circumstances faced by Sadie. You agree with the organisation to make joint representation to local councillors and the housing department, to explain your concerns and argue for improved housing provision, using real examples of hardship, such as Sadie's situation, to support your argument. You might also choose, as an individual rather than in your professional capacity, to write to a national paper, or to make approaches to your local MP and other national bodies, involved in the welfare of asylum-seekers. In this way, using your own knowledge, power and professional influence, where appropriate, you are challenging the status quo, and possibly contributing, through your own individual agency, to a more supportive and welcoming response to someone arriving in England and in need of asylum.

The idea that people can act on their own circumstances to bring about change, and can, perhaps, link up with others in the same situation and gain support and strength from each other, is of course not a new one and has been recognised by many practising in the helping professions (for example Beresford et al, 2006; Rowe, 2008). Effectively, what the members of these self-help groups are doing is refusing passively to accept their situation, but instead choosing to use their knowledge and experience to help themselves and others similarly affected. In doing so, they may help to bring about change and increased public awareness and understanding of the nature of their distress. This will be considered in more depth in Chapter Three.

Social workers as change agents

If we accept that an understanding of agency theory has worthwhile potential for social workers, then this has important implications for professionalism. Primarily, it supports and maintains the idea that both we as social workers and those with whom we work have the ability 'to make a difference to...a pre-existing state of affairs or course of events...that is, to exercise some sort of power' (Giddens, 1984, p 14); in fact, in recent years, there has been considerable discussion about developing practice and support for the notion of empowering service users. However, quite what they are being empowered to do and why has not received so much attention. Empowerment has instead simply been accepted as, self-evidently, a good thing. We will explore the concept of power more fully in the next chapter, but in the meantime, it is suggested that 'agency' is a more helpful concept to adopt. By using this term instead, the idea is introduced of service users taking action on their own behalf, behaving as authors and subjects of their own lives, believing that they have the power to make changes and make a difference, not only to their own lives but also to the very context within which they live. Indeed, it has been suggested that central to the idea of the self as agent is this belief, which in itself endows the believer with certain powers of action. In other words, confidence in one's own capacities is an essential prerequisite for the individual to exercise their own power. Without this confidence, the power remains latent (Harre, 1979, 1983). This belief is therefore, in itself, a cause for optimism and, when harnessed, is a powerful tool not only in the hands of service users but also for social workers. As has been noted, 'encouraging belief...is the most compelling consideration' (Stone, 1988, p 7, cited in Parton and O'Byrne, 2000, p 50).

As indicated in Chapter One, a number of contributions to social work theory have highlighted the significance of individual experience and identity. These include authors like Rogers writing from a client-centred perspective (Rogers, 1961), those from the interactionist school, such as Kelly (1955) and others representing the feminist approach, for example, Dominelli and McLeod (1989). All of these approaches have, in their various ways, focused on the reality of service-users' lives, on the importance of seeing the world through their eyes and of validating their point of view. Indeed, it is argued that unless we understand how individuals see the world, we will be unable usefully to interact with them.

The limitations of existing social work approaches

This focus on individual experience is fundamental to a social work that recognises the potential of individual agency, but, it is suggested, is not in itself sufficient. Specifically, it does not emphasise the additional possibility of individuals engaging with and influencing the structures that form the backdrop to their lives. In focusing primarily on the individual, these theorists fail to recognise the relationship that exists between agency and structure, of individuals using their transformative potential to bring about structural change. Later on in this chapter, we will be highlighting which social work methods can help to do this, using approaches that not only, in Parton and O'Byrne's words, identify agency, but also *amplify* it.

In focusing on the individual within their societal context and on how each can influence the other, the type of social work we are advocating has much in common with critical social work practice (Parton and O'Byrne, 2000; Fook, 2002/2006; Ferguson, 2008). Like some of these authors, we will be drawing on postmodern theory, and suggesting that there are multiple versions of the truth, of which none is transcendent. In terms of social work practice, there is therefore no one size that fits all. Instead, we will be suggesting that a focus on the particular experiences of service users and how this can be learned from and used in their own and others' interests, represents a more helpful approach.

Resilience, a 'sense of coherence' and identity

It will be helpful here to consider briefly a number of other concepts and their relevance to our subject. Resilience has been defined as 'a quality that helps individuals or communities resist or recover from adversities' (Newman, 2002) and, as such, is arguably central to agency. Rutter, for example, identifies human agency as being crucial in determining how children and adolescents cope with adversity, highlighting that what individuals bring to their experiences, is critical in terms of the outcome (Rutter, 2006). Significantly, he recognises that resilience is linked to external circumstances as well as to individual capacity, and that 'factors outside as well as within the individual needed to be considered' (Rutter, 1990, p 182). By implication then, Rutter is suggesting that a consideration of agency and structure, of the relationship between individuals and their environment, can provide a helpful context in which resilience can be better explored and understood. Kraemer similarly, writing about how to foster and promote resilience in children, suggests that it (resilience) is 'best understood as the experience of agency: that what you do or say makes a difference, that it is worthwhile making plans for your life, that you are not simply a helpless victim of forces beyond your control' (Kraemer, 1999, p 286). Additionally, Frost and Hoggett suggest that resilience can be described as 'a refusal to accept one's fate' (Frost and Hoggett, 2008, p 442). Self-belief, in other words, is not only central to agency but also to the concept of resilience, but in the absence of faith in oneself, any agency or power remains latent.

A 'sense of coherence' has been defined as the 'extent to which one sees one's world as comprehensible, manageable and meaningful' (Antonovsky, 1988, p 79). Antonovsky saw this sense of coherence as significant in terms of determining health, both mental and physical, and the ability to cope with stress. He also considered it critical to families' ability, or otherwise, to adapt to external change. Central to this sense of coherence is arguably also the idea of agency, of being able to shape one's own circumstances, of being in charge of one's own life, of being able to exercise influence over events. Since the areas of health, coping with stress and family adaptability form much of the substance of social work endeavour, the notion of a sense of coherence is also relevant in our consideration of agency and social work. We need therefore to find approaches and ways of working that build on and enhance this quality in our work with service users.

Similarly, it has been suggested that a sense of identity or self is a crucial component of mental health (Fook, 2002). Without an awareness of ourselves as unique individuals, with an idea of from where we come and of what we are capable, we run the risk of 'personal meaninglessness', of disconnection from society, of anomie (Giddens, 1991). In an era of rapid change such as our own, holding on to a sense of identity can represent a major challenge to anyone, but particularly to the more fragile and vulnerable members of society, who are likely to be among our service users. Acquiring a belief in one's own agency, a sense that we are not simply passive victims of whatever life throws at us, but able to act and resist, is therefore central to a notion of well-being, and something we need to try to foster in service users.

If we accept that resilience, a sense of coherence and identity are closely associated with the idea of agency, we need to consider how, as social workers, we can most effectively promote these factors in our work with service users. Focusing on examples from different user groups, we will now consider what methods might be helpful in this context.

Work with service users

Young children and children with disabilities

As social workers, we often need to engage with very young children and with those who have disabilities. This may be, for example, because children are subject to care proceedings and we need to ascertain their wishes and feelings. Alternatively, if they are disabled we may act as their key-worker, liaising with other professionals and trying to implement a plan that takes into account the needs and preferences of the child. In a more informal setting, working for example in a family centre on a council estate, we may be expected to organise group activities for children during school holidays. In all these situations, we need to be able to communicate effectively with children, to relate to them on their terms, and be seen as someone they can trust. So how do we set about this?

Advocates of play (Sylva, 1977; Gill, 1995; Balbernie, 1999) have long argued that adequate play provision and opportunities for play are crucial for children. This is for a number of reasons. Apart from the benefits for children's health, both emotional and physical, in terms of promoting physical activity and providing challenge and choice, play helps children learn and prepare, where appropriate, for school, by encouraging confidence, independence, curiosity and cooperation; and it encourages children to become sociable, to interact positively with their peers and with staff and to respect others. It also promotes the inclusion of children with disabilities in a straightforward and natural way and can lead to improved relationships between children (Sylva, 1977; Gill, 1995; Balbernie, 1999).

More recently, play activity between children and care-givers has been recognised as contributing to close attachment, which itself, can later influence adult mental health and well-being (for example Mental Health Foundation, 1999). Additionally, play proponents have long argued that in the UK, as opposed to most other European countries, children start school too young. They claim that beginning formal education too soon is counterproductive, that children need longer to enjoy undirected play activity, and that they learn more from this than from more formal settings. They claim that 'play is the child's work', a statement attributed to Maria Montessori (1870–1952) and children should be allowed to learn in their own way. The Labour administration has recently recognised some of these arguments. Not only have they introduced a national Play Strategy (DCSF, 2008) but the Early Years curriculum has also changed in emphasis and now contains requirements in relation to play, including the provision of opportunities for outdoor play.

There is, however, another advantage to play. Winn points out that play provides a vehicle for children to become participants in situations of their own choosing, to take an active role in their own lives as opposed to mere recipients of actions done to them (Winn, 2002). It provides, in other words, an opportunity for children to experience a sense of mastery, to begin to exercise choice and be active in influencing and controlling their external environment, to start to grow up, in other words, with a sense of their own agency. We can easily recognise the benefits for children who from an early age are cared for by people who treat them as individuals, respect their choices and accept their right to hold views that are different from their own. These are the children who most often grow up with a sense of self-belief and worth, who go on to achieve greater things and to fulfil their ambitions. Others, however, grow up in very different and far less favourable circumstances, and it is these children that we are most likely to encounter in our work. By promoting play activities, by offering them opportunities to choose, to shape their experience and influence what happens around them, we can perhaps help them begin to feel a measure of power and self-worth, and start to foster a sense of resilience and autonomy in these children.

Young offenders

For teams involved with children and families, work with adolescents often forms a significant part of their caseload. Young people who start to offend may come from families where other difficulties have already been identified; or they may be referred in their own right, their behaviour being the first sign that all is not well. Often, their offending is the first step such children and young people take on the road into the 'looked after' or care system, and indeed may represent the beginning of a life of crime. How we relate to them, the choices made both by the young person, their families and ourselves, and how they are dealt with by the courts is therefore of great importance in terms of influencing their future life chances. We discussed in the first chapter, how, in compiling a pre-sentence report, a worker can choose to focus on what are perceived as the social or structural determinants of the young person's behaviour – local unemployment figures and the family's associated poverty, for example – or may seek to highlight the youngster's individual attributes and behaviour, and the meaning that this particular offence holds for them. In the latter instance, we are trying to convey to the court a sense of the offender as a real person; to say, in the words of Foucault, that 'behind the offender...stands the delinquent' (Foucault, 2004, p 371). In other words, he is an individual who has a separate existence from his offence, and is the author or agent of his own acts, for whom they have some meaning.

To understand this, however, we need to know and understand the young person or agent himself. For the offender, it may be that life does seem to hold very few choices, that offending or touting drugs, and their perceived (and, in the case of drugs, financially very real) rewards, seem the logical way out of a situation where the alternative is either unemployment or work that is poorly paid, insecure, or mind-numbingly repetitive. But we would be wrong to assume this, or to believe that we know what the young person in question is thinking about his circumstances. What we need to do is to find a way for the youngster to clarify for himself and us what meaning his behaviour holds, and then to engage with him on these terms.

An example of a positive approach to engaging with young offenders

Teenagers and young people are often poor communicators at the best of times and talking to a social worker is likely to be much harder for them. An interest, however, in computers or drama, for instance, might indicate possible ways of engaging with a young service user. It may be suggested, for instance, that they would like to interview themselves, and record this 'two-way' conversation. As their social worker, you could offer examples of various questions they might use, beginning with the more straightforward and moving on to the more probing and personal. Assuming they are prepared to share the resulting tape or video with you, this could prove a helpful route into what is important to them and how they are thinking and provide a basis for future discussion. This approach draws on the personal construct work of Kelly, described earlier, and may also involve the use of repertory grids completed on the computer (cf. Fransella and Dalton, 1990). Such grids offer a way of measuring, through simple replicable techniques, how a young person constructs their view of the world, what is important to them, and which factors might contribute to their decision-making. Through interpretation of these grids, service users can come to identify their own version of reality, determine their own scale of priorities, and start to make life choices based on these criteria. These methods can, in addition, help avoid the pitfalls that occur when social worker and offender do not share a common value system, when goals identified by professionals do not correspond with those of the young person, for whom they may have little or no relevance. These in turn could help the offender to examine his own constructs, to attempt to explain his behaviour to himself, and, in turn, enable you to explore your service user's world through his eyes. Through this exercise, the young person may, in discussion, find alternative ways of looking at his circumstances, and work out how to change them. Indeed, 'the essential message...of personal construct psychology (PCP) ...is that change is always possible for any client' (Fransella and Dalton, 1990, p 4); or as Kelly himself put it, 'no one needs paint himself into a corner; no one needs to be completely hemmed in by circumstances; no one needs to be the victim of his biography' (Kelly, 1955, p 15).

The congruence between personal construct psychology and building up a sense of agency will be self-evident here. What is important is that by coming to believe that change is possible, that things could be otherwise, the young person is enabled, *if he chooses*, to move from a state of passive victimhood, to one where he can move from the sense of being an object, to experiencing himself as the subject or author of his own life, where he can experience a sense of control and ultimately a feeling of responsibility towards himself and others.

There are, however, a number of important issues to stress here. First, for the young person to make positive changes to her life and in her behaviour, she has to believe that change is possible. Belief, both in oneself and in the potential for things to be otherwise, is, as we have tried to indicate, central to the exercise of agency. Part of the role of the worker in this situation then is to encourage the young person in whatever way possible to have faith in themselves, and their own potential for doing things differently; to imagine an alternative world for themselves, to think how this would feel and consider how it might be achieved. As has been suggested, 'an account of potential sources of change is vital...for professionals and clients in search of resources and hope' (Batsleer and Humphreys, 2000, p 15). An underlying lack of self-confidence, perhaps surprisingly, often goes with the territory of offending behaviour, and this will need challenging and the young person supported at every point as they try to make changes. The use of reparation, where offenders, with support from relevant professionals, make some compensation to their victims, may have a place here, and encourage the offender who genuinely regrets his offences to feel that he can move forward and change the way he sees himself and is viewed by others. Social pedagogy, with its central concerns of well-being and happiness, might also provide a helpful context in which to engage with young offenders. This approach will be considered in more depth in Chapter Four.

Second, the offender needs to decide that he wants to change. This is by no means a given: indeed, if it were this simple, offending would now very probably be a thing of the past. Realistically, not all young people are going to change their behaviour, however appropriate and sensitive the methods employed to engage with them, and many may simply opt to carry on as before. What they will be doing instead is effectively exercising what has been termed 'negative agency' (Stenner and Taylor, 2008, p 433), where feelings of passivity, self-destructiveness or simply a lack of desire to behave in more socially acceptable ways, are or remain paramount. Essentially, they will still be actors, behaving more or less rationally, but their choices will be directed more towards retaining the status quo than to seeking to change it. It may well be, for example, that the income and peer-status derived from drug-dealing or robbery is so seductive that a young offender makes a clear decision to continue on his offending path. In these circumstances, his decision has, in the end, to be respected.

Third, it would be instructive to consider in more depth why it is that some young people in a given set of circumstances choose to offend, while others in similar situations do not. Why, in other words, are some young people more resilient in the face of adversity and what can we learn from their background and early childhood experiences that might be of assistance in our work with other young people? Similarly, in the knowledge that 80% of young people released from young offender institutions go on to commit further offences (Bateman, 2006, p 74) it might be helpful to try to discover from the remaining 20% why, in their cases, they choose not to do so.

Finally, despite the emphasis here on the offender being encouraged to exercise agency, and to do so in a positive rather than a negative manner making whatever changes they can, it is also part of the social work role to recognise the structural constraints on a young person's behaviour. They need to acknowledge their difficult circumstances and the societal forces – their poverty, poor housing and lack of available job opportunities, for example – that are beyond his individual control. They may reflect on the fact that New Labour has created 3,000 new offences since assuming power in 1997 (Morris, 2006). They might also bear in mind the peculiarly British structural constraint of the age of criminal responsibility being as low as 10. This is at odds with virtually the whole of the rest of Europe and serves to 'criminalise' a far higher number of young people in our society. Using their own sense of agency to challenge the status quo, part of a social worker's overall responsibility should be to represent the realities of their service users' lives to those who can make a difference to them, to local councillors and to national politicians. As people who perhaps have unique access to these realities, they are in the optimum position to seek to initiate change, where they can see that this is required.

Work with families

Family work comprises much of the workload of many social workers and a great deal has been written about the various approaches that can be adopted, ranging from systemic family therapy (for example Walrond-Skinner, 1976; Skynner and Cleese, 1983) to family support methods and the use of neighbourhood children and family centres (for example Frost et al, 2003; Butt and Box, 1998). Perhaps with no other group of service users, however, is it more important to understand the world as they and individual family members themselves perceive it. As Tolstoy famously said, 'All happy families are the same, but every unhappy family is unhappy in its own way,' (Tolstoy, 1878) and as it is with these unhappy families that social workers habitually engage, we need to attempt to unravel and understand their individual experience of unhappiness.

The language sometimes used to describe families who are users of services is significant here. They may be referred to, in the media or by politicians, for example, as socially excluded, as deviant and feckless, or as 'problem families'. It is their children who are most often subject to neglect, who are more likely to cause trouble at school, who will become offenders and be unemployed, whose outcomes will, in other words, be in one way or another 'negative'.

The labelling of some young people in recent years as 'hoodies' is a case in point here. Merely referring to groups of young people in this way serves in some way to dehumanise them, to foster a sense in the wider community that they are 'different', in the wrong by virtue of their clothing alone, and more likely to offend. Such a view fails to recognise that, in the eyes of the young people themselves, they may simply be enjoying being sociable with their friends, choosing to wear clothes that identify them as a group, in much the same way as, for example, adults dressing for a particular sport.

Labelling families and children in this way serves to objectify them, to see them as 'other' and unlike ourselves, who are fortunate enough to be among the socially *in*cluded. These families and young people are seen as differing from an assumed norm, and the labelling process, in itself, tends to deny the possibility of change. Put somewhat differently, service users or 'welfare subjects' are characterised as 'dependent, unpredictable, unable to act in their own interests, lacking agency' (Frost and Hoggett, 2008, p 439). Crucially, such language suggests that these people, unlike those ascribing the labels, are powerless, able to do nothing to influence their situation. They need instead to be managed, supervised or controlled, encouraged to fit in and conform, but are viewed pessimistically as unlikely to do so, at least without a great deal of costly input from statutory services.

Those who are in this situation may in turn see themselves as powerless, lacking in choice, with whatever self-determination they possess being taken up with coping and surviving (Frost and Hoggett, 2008, p 441). They will in a sense see themselves as objects, rather than as the subject of their own lives, lacking the capacity to act on their situation and bring about change. This is all the more likely where their background and experiences have fostered a sense of passivity, of 'learned helplessness' (Seligman, 1975). Frost and Hoggett (2008) describe this as 'social suffering', where the 'social damage inflicted...on the least powerful... their "inner worlds of psychic suffering and outer worlds of social structural oppression" make up these subjects and influence their degree of agency' (p 440).

It would be wrong, however, to consider this as the only possibility. Not all those who live in what others may perceive as difficult circumstances view their own lives in this way. They may not even recognise this description of their lives. As Jean Bartlett, a resident of the Aylesbury Estate in South London, said recently, in response to descriptions of her area being like, among other things, 'hell's waiting room' (*Daily Mail,* cited by McSmith, 2008), 'You're stigmatised if you live on a council estate.... We find it unfair that the media always come here and think we're so bloody deprived. We're not' (Muir, 2005). Even those who do view their circumstances in negative terms may not accept their lot passively, considering that they can exert little or no influence over their circumstances. Although 'modern life impoverishes individual action' (Giddens, 1991) there are those who 'react against social circumstances which they find oppressive' and 'engage boldly with the outer social world' (Giddens, 1991, p 175). These are people who possess a degree of resilience, who believe that things can be otherwise and that they themselves can effect change. They do not feel like victims of fate, despite their situation.

So, in this context, how can we, as social workers, engage with families and help them achieve change? How do we promote their resilience and a sense of at least partial control over their circumstances?

Social workers and statutory powers

First of all, we need to consider how families are likely to come to our attention as social workers. In today's social work climate, the reality is that they will probably be referred as in need of support, without which, or if they fail to engage with us, there is a risk that their children may be removed. We are cast, in this situation more than perhaps any other in social work, in the role of agents of social control, representatives of the social structures that society has mandated us to uphold. Against this background, we are unlikely to be viewed in positive terms by parents and children, who are likely at the very least to be fearful of us, and quite possibly to present as angry at our intervention and resistant to any suggestions we may have to make. How then do we intervene and attempt to move things on in a positive direction?

The issue of power is central here. In these situations, parents and children will see social workers as possessing enormous powers, far more than we ourselves may feel that we have. Indeed, as has been noted, social workers tend to feel responsible but relatively power*less*, accepting responsibility but feeling unable to change the situation (Fook, 2002). Looked at from an agentic perspective, however, it is possible to recognise that not only do we as social workers exercise considerable power, consciously or otherwise, but also those with whom we work actually possess some of their own, whether or not they are aware of it. Indeed, it may be that they are using it merely to cope, to get by (Lister, 2004) or to challenge those like ourselves, especially those of us from statutory agencies and who have authority in relation to certain aspects of their lives. In these potentially fraught situations then, it is our role as social workers, to help service users realise that they do have a degree of power, that they can choose how to use it, and can begin to exercise some control over their own lives. In other words, once they believe it is possible, they themselves can start to bring about change.

So how do we approach families in these situations and what methods should we adopt? It is generally accepted that most parents want the best for their children, aspire to be good enough parents, and wish to care for them and bring them up themselves. Similarly, the majority of children would prefer, if possible, to remain living at home. However, there will always, unfortunately, be some situations where home is not a safe place for children and they need to be protected and looked after away from their family. Statutory intervention is ultimately needed in these instances to protect both the child and their parents and in this situation, the demands of society for safety and protection will supersede the needs of service users to exercise agency. Where and how this line is drawn is crucial.

Before this point is reached, however, there are methods that may hopefully reduce the need for statutory intervention. One such approach is solution-focused therapy or the strengths–based approach to working with families. This approach has been described as a whole philosophy, one that takes as its starting point the belief that people hold the seeds of solution inside themselves (Parton and O'Byrne, 2000). These authors, presenting their case for 'constructive social work', suggest that people are not always aware of what they know until their knowledge is activated in a way that makes a difference and 'their self-agency is empowered' (Parton and O'Byrne, 2000, p 111). Using this approach, service users are encouraged to externalise their problems, to see their behaviour as something separate from themselves, which they are not personally defined by and over which they can exercise some control. The use of language is central here, with the emphasis needing to be placed on what the individual herself has done, rather than what has happened to them, to recast them as active agents rather than passive victims. By emphasising individuals' behaviour in this way, they can, over time, come to believe that things could be otherwise, that they need not be cast permanently in the role of victim, but can choose to behave differently and hence bring about changes and different outcomes. Parents facing the possibility of care proceedings, for example, might therefore be encouraged to imagine a more positive future, one where their children will remain at home and where social workers will no longer be involved. What changes they need to make will, of course, have to be openly acknowledged, with this, in itself, beginning to reduce the imbalance of power and bringing the situation more within their control. The focus will always rest on what strengths the family can demonstrate, and how these can be built on and maximised in future. As Parton and O'Byrne observe, 'Linked to strength is personal agency. Discussing how a person manages to do something difficult, how they create exceptions, how they choose what is good for them, not only builds up the sense of self-power but also the *awareness* of ability and strength' (Parton and O'Byrne, 2000, p 72). What is important is that this approach also implies an underlying respect for the service user, and a belief in their potential to change and help themselves. This in turn will be conveyed to them and reinforce their own sense of worth and self-respect.

Another way of working with families that conveys respect for them as a group and seeks to find a way forward from within the family's own resources is through the use of Family Group Conferences. This method is effectively a means of sharing power with the family and putting them at the centre of the action and the decision-making process. Where, for example, parents are demonstrably unable safely to care for their children themselves, the conference process may identify members of the extended family who share the professionals' concerns and are prepared to take on the parenting task themselves. Similarly, where a young person's behaviour may be escalating into difficulties at school or with the police, and the parents are unable or unwilling to exert control over him or her, grandparents, or others within the family network may put themselves forward as alternative carers who are acceptable to all parties concerned. Even in the most intractable of situations, this approach has often proved successful and been able to demonstrate, not only to professionals, but, what is more important, to the family themselves that they possess their own strengths as a family unit, that these can be built on and that they can act creatively to bring about their own solutions. Effectively, the whole family is empowered and retains control over its own affairs (see Hudson and Galloway, 1996).

What we as social workers must never forget, however, in our work with families, is the reality of the objective difficulties they so often face. As people who are privileged to have access to their lives, and hence to witness the poverty and desperate housing conditions which they often have to endure, the lack of access to shops, banks and utilities that most of us take for granted, we need also to do all we can to address these injustices. We can, for example, ensure that service users are claiming all the benefits to which they are entitled, make collective approaches to housing officials and, within our own departments and organisations, argue for services that better meet their needs. In this way, we will be using what power we have, as our service users' representatives, to bring about structural change where necessary, and to challenge the view that all problems are rooted in individual behaviour.

People with mental health problems

It has been suggested that mental illness represents an unwillingness to conform to some of what life demands from the individual (Goffman, 1962). Here, Goffman is viewing mental ill-health from the patient's point of view, and hence primarily as a state of mind experienced subjectively. Society, however, in dealing with those who are mentally ill, tends to objectify them, almost to the exclusion, arguably, of allowing them subjective status at all. This is where, as Philp recognises, social work potentially has much to offer, through encouraging a view of service users that emphasises their individuality and subjective status. As he writes, 'the social worker cannot help but try to create people, subjects, where everyone else is seeing cold, hard, objective facts' (Philp, 1979, p 99). She (the social worker) is trying to make real to others 'the underlying character, the hidden depths, the essential good, the authentic and the unalienated' (Philp, 1979, p 99). She is trying, in other words, to encourage others to recognise the shared humanity of the mentally-ill service user.

That social work is well placed to recognise the uniqueness of individuals and represent their experiences to others is recognised similarly elsewhere (Williams et al, 1999). These authors note, however, that in reality social workers often fall down in this respect. It is perhaps never more important than in the mental health field, however, that social workers do succeed in conveying to others – to psychiatrists, lawyers and doctors – the subjective nature of service users' experiences, in order that we respond to them sensitively and constructively. For, as Riessmann states, 'it is in the interpretation of an event by the social actor that significance may lie, and consequently the potential for distress and disorder' (Riessman, cited in Williams et al, 1999, p 88).

In our role as social workers, we need also to challenge the type of thinking that this treatment of mentally-ill people represents; that sees the world in terms of dichotomies, where one category is defined negatively in relation to the other, where people are viewed as 'good/bad', 'better/worse', and 'sane/insane', with the inevitable effect of marginalising and excluding those, such as mental health sufferers, who are seen as different from the norm. Indeed, as we have highlighted, postmodern theory encourages a belief in multiple meanings, of 'situated subjectivity', where an individual's own sense of self is multifaceted, constantly changing and precarious. As Fook observes 'this...potentially empowers previously marginal people, because it acknowledges and legitimises their experiences and identities. It...allows for more complex forms of theory to be developed...making for...potentially more flexible practice...and new forms of empowerment' (Fook, 2002, p 14).

A sense of identity or self is, as we have noted crucial to mental health (Fook, 2002). Drawing on ideas of 'narrative' originally developed by Giddens (1991), Sands (1996, cited in Fook, 2002, p 75) introduces the idea of 'narrative identity', where individuals can integrate possibly adverse experiences into a coherent sense of whole, where the story created can have a cause as well as an effect, and where the possibility of change according to personal experience can restore a sense of agency to the individual. As noted earlier, this 'sense of coherence' is critical in managing stress and adapting to external change, issues that pose particular problems for those with mental health difficulties. The idea of narrative is also recognised as important by Giddens for whom it is at the core of self-identity in the modern world (Giddens, 1991).

So, if a sense of narrative identity is so important to mental health, how do we, as social workers, promote this in our work with service users? In the 1970s and 1980s, 'narrative therapy' was developed in Australia and New Zealand by Michael White (for example, White and Epston, 1990). He applied Giddens' ideas of individual narratives to different user groups, to those, for example, suffering from anorexia nervosa or schizophrenia, and through the use of narrative, sought to translate personal experience into stories, which in turn revealed the way people made meaning out of their lives. In doing so, this also effectively externalised the problem, attributing the cause or blame to factors outside the individual and located in oppressive social structures. The very process of helping service users construct new narratives can, it is suggested, introduce them to new ways of viewing their situation, and help them build a stronger sense of identity. By moving to the use of the active rather than the passive voice, to accepting responsibility rather than attributing blame, and through emphasising strengths rather than weaknesses, individuals can build a stronger sense of identity and increase their individual sense of power and agency.

An example of this approach in practice, is the emergence in the 1990s, of the Hearing Voices Network. This was initially developed in Holland, by a psychiatrist and service user (Romme and Escher, 1993), and effectively challenges the dominant discourse that interprets such behaviour as symptomatic of mental ill-health, as a reason to label someone as 'mad' or schizophrenic. Instead, those who hear voices are encouraged to see this as an unusual perceptual experience, and to put time aside to listen to and interpret what the voices are saying to them. In this sense, they re-define themselves as active agents, whose unusual experiences are meaningful and important to them and over which they exercise some personal control. In doing so, they are also challenging the psychiatric definition of hearing voices, and redefining their experiences as normal. They are, in addition, re-interpreting themselves as powerful rather than powerless in relation to their experiences and, through this, fostering their own sense of identity and coherence (for example Bentall, 1990; Brown, 2001). The significance of this movement, which is now user-led, will be examined more fully in the next chapter.

Narrative therapy also provides a potentially helpful way of working with those in other negatively defined situations, for example vulnerable older people and those who are dying. This will also be addressed in the next chapter.

Further implications for social work

The approaches outlined thus far in this chapter share a number of common features, which it will be helpful to identify. First, they all emphasise the significance of self-belief – the awareness that by using their own agency and power, service users can bring about change and make an impact on their circumstances and on the people around them. This is true of very young children, through their play activities, of those with disabilities, and of those viewed by mainstream society as 'different' or deviant. Everybody, in other words, by imagining that things could be otherwise and acting on this belief, can begin to exercise greater control over their own lives, and also to influence the context in which these lives are lived. We all possess agency, and in becoming aware of this, can choose to use this for positive ends.

It is important to remember, however, that agency is not necessarily always used constructively. This may be true, for example, of offenders, abusers, and those suffering from mental illness, groups who may choose to use their agency to what may seem to others, very negative effect. A young offender, for example, may simply opt, for whatever reason, not to change his deviant behaviour. In making this choice, he is arguably acting agentically, but doing so self-destructively and the result may be, for him, a prison sentence. As Hoggett observed, 'there is a possibility that some parts of the personality may be actively engaged in a destructive relationship with other parts' and 'a full picture of human agency must keep in touch with this tragic dimension' (Hoggett, 2001, p 47).

Second, the people who possess this self-belief are typically those who might be described as resilient, who have a greater sense of coherence and a stronger feeling of identity. These are people who are more able to withstand difficult circumstances, who, faced with adversity, are not overwhelmed by it, do not experience the 'collapse of agency' that depression represents (Hoggett, 2001, p 47), but are more able to resist and challenge their circumstances. As Giddens points out, we need to learn from those who are resilient, and what enables them to be so (Giddens, 1991). In our work then, we need to adopt the sorts of approaches outlined above, ones that emphasise not only that change happens, but also that we ourselves can influence how it comes about. By these means, we will be fostering our clients' resilience, enhancing their own sense of coherence and identity and opening up their potential to resist and challenge (Fook, 2002).

Third, in order to promote this way of working, we need to resist the definition of ourselves, currently put forward by both major political parties, as mere agents of social control. Whilst this is undeniably a part of our role, the characterisation of social work in these terms does a major disservice to the profession, encouraging as it does a misplaced view both that service users can and should be subject to control and that we are the people best-placed to carry out this function. This perception moreover actually militates against our therapeutic potential in terms of enhancing our clients' sense of agency, an aspect of our work that depends on skills that are arguably at odds with those involved in monitoring and surveillance.

Agency and relationship

These skills are most apparent in the final point to be made here. For the approaches identified in this chapter to succeed, they all presuppose a positive working relationship between ourselves and our service users. Agency, after all, assumes relationship (Parton and O'Byrne, 2000) and it is within relationships that power lies (Giddens, 1979). For service users to trust us and for us even to begin to try and understand the reality of their lives, we need to build up a sense of partnership with them – a feeling that we are collaborating on a shared enterprise and that we care about them and what they can achieve. And this does not happen overnight. Relationships take time to form, and trust can be very hard to establish. Claire Allan, writing about her experiences as a long-term mental health service user, talks movingly about her relationship with her social worker, 'a celebration' as she describes it, 'of the possibilities of the social worker/client relationship'. She talks of her social worker's sincerity and commitment, 'her utter reliability, showing up week after week...the consummate patience, the sheer amount of time B. was willing to offer' which was 'critical in building the trust we needed to work together'. She talks, too, of being 'an active participant in my own recovery...but it was B. who enabled me to engage in the process, who made my recovery possible' (Allan, 2009). Through this highly significant relationship, Claire had, in other words, effectively come to believe in and experience a sense of her own agency. For change to be possible in those who suffer from the kinds of serious difficulties experienced by Claire, this process cannot be short-changed and we need to be aware of how crucial a positive and enduring relationship is to any success. Whatever the economic context of our work, relationships are one thing that cannot and should not be cut back.

So what does all this mean for us as social workers? We need, primarily, to be mindful that social work is, as Parton and O'Byrne recognise, a moral activity (Parton and O'Byrne, 2000) and be aware that we cannot approach it as 'just another job'. This means that in our work with service users, we need to remain aware that each individual is unique and respect and honour their reality, resisting those theories and practices that suggest or infer that 'one way fits all'. We need, in other words, to challenge the 'false universalism' that characterised the post-war welfare state (Ferguson, 2008) and emphasise the 'particular' that we recognise in our clients' experiences, acknowledging that there are different versions of the truth. In doing so, however, we must oppose the idea that 'there is no such thing as society' (Thatcher, 1987). We must not take the view that, in believing in client self-determination, in people's capacity to exercise agency and shape their circumstances, that they are therefore always responsible and open to blame when things go wrong (Stenner and Taylor, 2008). On the contrary, we need, Janus-like, to face both ways; to use the fact that we operate in the intermediate zone between the state and the private sphere of the household – the space in-between – and recognise that our role is to mediate between the excluded and the mainstream (Parton and O'Byrne, 2000).

Moreover, if we accept that service users possess power and are able to exercise this, we need to model this behaviour ourselves by recognising and using our own sense of agency. In our pivotal position, mediating between the service user and society, we need to use our own transformative capacity to not only 'feel the pain of the other and think critically about the injustices that produce it' (Frost and Hoggett, 2008, p 455), but, as suggested earlier, to use our own understanding of service users' lives to try to reduce those injustices. We need to find ways to convey the reality of their experiences, both to our own managers and directors, and also to political leaders, as appropriate, to negotiate about budgets, to challenge cutbacks, to resist managerial emphases on outcomes that measure, not what clients see as important to them, but indices that relate more to bureaucratic priorities.

To achieve this, we need a much greater focus on service user participation, on helping those with whom we work to achieve a position where they are co-producers of services, ones that are shaped, delivered and controlled in accordance with their own needs. We will discuss this in the next chapter where the notion of empowerment will be considered more fully. We will also explore the concepts of capacity-building and citizenship and the rights and obligations that flow from them.

THREE

Service users as co-producers of services

'How many social workers does it take to change a light bulb?' 'None, but the light bulb has to believe it can change.' (Anon)

Treat a man the way he is and he will remain so. Treat a man the way he can be and ought to be, and he will become as he can and should be. (Goethe)

Introduction

In Chapter Two, we highlighted the importance to social work of an understanding of agency theory and its centrality to any concept of change. We explored a number of concepts and their relevance to our subject and went on to consider a variety of approaches and methods that might enhance the agency of groups of service users, ranging from young children involved in play, to families and those with mental health problems. Finally, we identified the significance of certain common features, such as promoting self-belief, enhancing resilience and the quality of relationships, that are central to all the approaches outlined, as well as the need for us, as social workers, to recognise the moral nature of our work, to nurture a sense of our own agency, and to consider how best we can use this to the benefit of service users.

In this chapter, we will be taking a closer look at the concept of empowerment. We will compare it with the idea of agency and consider why agency can serve our purposes more effectively. We will then attempt to apply this theory to social work practice and consider how, through consultation, participation, service user involvement and the co-production of services, power can be shared and promoted. We will also reflect on the notion of citizenship and how this fits into our thinking.

Finally, we will explore the idea of 'the other' and note how, in acting agentically, individuals and groups who are seen in this light can challenge the status quo and change our perceptions, and our ways of viewing both them and ourselves.

To begin with, however, and to serve as an introduction to the issues that this chapter will address, we will briefly consider the issue of dying and terminal care, and how, even at this stage of their life, an individual can exercise agency and choice.

The act of dying

One example of individuals engaging creatively with life and making plans that contain meaning for them on a personal level is the way that, given the opportunity, they might choose, paradoxically, to die. Dying is, without doubt, the most intensely personal experience that we, as human beings face, one of the 'givens' of our existence, a social fact over which, with the exception of suicide, we exercise no personal control. It is the only one, moreover, other than being born, that we go through totally alone, and our own birth is not an experience, thankfully, on which we are able to reflect! As Eliot observed in 'Sweeney Agonistes':

> Birth, and copulation and death,
> That's all the facts when you come to brass tacks. (T.S. Eliot)

Huxley observed in *The doors of perception*, that 'The martyrs go hand in hand into the arena; they are crucified alone' (Huxley, 1954, p 6).

It is not the facts of birth and death but only the life in-between which, by implication, holds individual meaning and significance. This is a view traditionally reinforced by Christianity, where believers are encouraged to view death, and the manner in which it occurs, as subject to the will of God, rather than man. So death comes 'like a thief in the night' at a time of God's choosing, with Christians encouraged to pin their hopes in 'the life hereafter'.

To describe dying as an 'act' might, therefore, on first consideration, seem rather strange. Surely, it might be said, death is something that just happens to people, not something which contains any element of intentionality. And this is of course true in many circumstances, particularly when people die suddenly or prematurely, in an accident for example, or from a sudden heart attack. But although death, as the natural end of life is itself inescapable, how we die is something over which we can, in fact, often exercise some control.

One example of this, of course, lies in the act of committing or attempting to commit suicide. In doing so, the individual is arguably saying that he wishes to shed responsibility for her life: since life and the ability to exercise free will and freedom of choice have become too much for her to bear, she is trying to and believes she is succeeding in suspending her own agency. By committing suicide, however, she is in fact, arguably making the most clear-cut, agentic response possible to the state of uncertainty or unhappiness that she is confronting. This meaning is clear when, for example, someone who is faced with imminent death, or the prospect of continuing life after the death of a much-loved partner, chooses suicide as a means of release.

Those who are told that they have a terminal illness commonly react with a sense of shock and disbelief, often accompanied by a feeling of powerlessness. Life assumes a dreamlike quality, where events simply happen, rather than being brought about by some action or intent on the part of the individual. In this state, a patient may become very suggestible, and more open than usual to advice from others. In surrendering responsibility to this extent to other people, she gives up some control over her life and, in doing so, makes it more likely that any future choices will be influenced or taken by people other than herself. In other words, as her life approaches its end, she may well have less and less opportunity to act agentically. This situation may indeed be compounded in an institutional setting such as a hospital, particularly where death is seen as a failure on the part of the medical profession, and postponed for as long as possible, at the expense of quality of life. This 'banishment' of the dying to hospital and the idea of death representing failure is addressed by Aries, who suggests that in current Western society we are now less afraid and more ashamed of death, behaving as if it did not exist (Aries, 1981). In those hospitals where patients are still given little information about their illness and its possible treatment, they are not in a position to make considered decisions about how they will die and their degree of agency is very low. As a cancer patient, writing of his experiences, explains, 'Even in the best hospitals, the loss of freedom and dependence on anonymous forces can be oppressive' (Marqusee, 2009).

It has been observed that those cancer patients who died soon after diagnosis were those 'stricken by a sense of powerlessness and who have little motivation to live' (Simonton, 1978, cited in Tatchell, 1986). Conversely, those who survived against medical odds had 'a firm belief that they could influence the course of their illness' (Simonton, 1978). In these situations, where power was effectively handed back to patients and shared with them, it enabled them to exercise choice, to resume some responsibility and control for the remaining part of their lives, and in many cases even to influence the manner of their eventual dying. Indeed, not only was agency restored to them, but by using the transformative capacity of their collective power, these patients and others like them have arguably helped to influence the way in which society and its institutions now generally perceive and deal far more sensitively with death and with those who are currently dying. They provide, in other words, an important example of the dynamic interplay between individuals and society – of how agency can influence structures, even at the point of death. Kubler-Ross has in fact, referred to dying as a learning process, through which many people become able, for the first time, to take responsibility for their own lives (Kubler-Ross, 1975), and ultimately may have a positive influence on the way in which others die in future.

Empowerment

We have already acknowledged some difficulties associated with the concept of empowerment and suggested that agency might be a more helpful term to adopt. We will now move on to consider why this might be the case, bearing in mind the example that we have just considered of how some people can and do choose to die.

In the last twenty years, social work has focused increasingly on the need for practice to empower service users. This term has had such a 'feel-good' factor that its meaning has rarely, until recently, been fully analysed and challenged. Instead, it has been taken for granted that empowerment must, of necessity, be a good thing, and in the interests of service users. Far from being the radical way forward that is often supposed, however, it can also have politically conservative overtones (Fook, 2002). If, for example, we now examine this term more closely, it is salient to ask who is being empowered, by whom and, what is most important, in whose interests and on whose terms.

Returning to the ideas put forward in previous chapters, we will recall the distinction that was made between people who are the subjects of their own lives, who are in the position of being able to make active decisions about how they live, and those who can be seen merely as objects, whose lives are lived out on other people's terms, especially those of the people who effectively wield power over them. Within a social work context, however, as Philp noted, service users are not traditionally granted subjective status, and instead it is their objective status that is highlighted (Philp, 1979). A first difficulty with the notion of empowerment then, is that individuals are not perceived as subjects or agents of their own destiny, but rather as objects of another group's concerns. It is those who already enjoy subjective status who decide on what terms others should be empowered, who are effectively 'doing' something to those other people who are perceived as objects, in this case service users.

An example of parent empowerment (1)

Local authority 'A' decides that it wants to empower local parents. They draw up a Parents' Charter, advising parents of their rights and committing the various local authority departments to their delivery. This is done in all good faith, with those concerned sincerely committed to improving the lot of local parents. What happens, however, is that parents measure their circumstances against what is on offer, rather than considering what they, as parents, might like to see in place and engaging in some 'blue sky thinking'. The effect is that services are left much the same; they are merely tinkered with around the edges.

In this example, even if new services are introduced, the status quo remains effectively unchallenged, the structure remains the same and those already enjoying power continue to do so, and remain in charge. The apparent empowerment of those with objective status is therefore, in this respect, largely illusory.

A second difficulty with the notion of empowerment lies in its reductionist qualities. When we talk of empowering people, it is usual to do so in terms of group membership. So, for example, we tend to speak of the empowerment of black people, of women or of those with disabilities. In doing so, we are identifying individuals by characteristics that they themselves may or may not find meaningful. For an African-Caribbean man, for instance, his skin colour may be far less important to him than the fact that his family background is Kenyan rather than Ethiopian, or that he is a Manchester United, rather than a Manchester City supporter; and rather than her sex, it may, at certain times, be more significant to a woman that she is a teacher or an NHS employee, and actually unhelpful and disempowering to her to focus on her gender. Either way, it is often the group membership of individuals that is emphasised by those seeking to empower them, rather than what they are unto themselves, with their individual interests, ideas and identity subsumed into a larger, and possibly, to them, irrelevant whole. By reducing individuals to one or perhaps several characteristics they are ironically, therefore, being in some ways disempowered and potentially alienated from other, perhaps to them more important aspects of their lives. Moreover, in being objectified in this way, their behaviour is seen again as determined by external, societal forces; as individuals they are, to quote Garfinkel's term again, mere 'cultural dopes' (Garfinkel, 1967). Empowerment on these terms, in failing to move beyond the ascription of often irrelevant labels, therefore runs the risk of being at best patronising and at worst meaningless.

Third, as Fook points out, to attribute the label of powerlessness to a group of people can, itself, be disempowering (Fook, 2002). It assumes that people fall into two categories, the 'powerful' and the 'powerless', with the latter group seen as weak and cast in the role of victims. For the former group to decide that power should be redistributed, their perceptions will inevitably take priority. So for those seen as powerless, 'the experience of being given power may not be experienced as empowering, but in fact may have disempowering effects' (Fook, 2002, p 51, cited in R. Smith, 2008, p 37). Moreover, for those who perceive themselves as powerless to seek to become powerful, suggests that it is in the interests of the former group to aspire to be like those who hold power at present, which, in turn, further devalues the reality of those who lack it. It may indeed lead to the situation where the oppressed ultimately become the oppressors, the bullied become the bullies, or children who are subjected to overly harsh parenting regimes, grow up to be punitive parents themselves. It is arguably far more helpful to recognise that 'every person...exercises and has the potential to create some form of power...The key to understanding power...is...to appreciate how it is expressed, experienced and created by different people at different levels' (Fook, 2002, p 52). In short, empowerment is, as has been suggested, 'too vague, woolly and ambiguous a concept' to be helpful and, moreover, 'vulnerable to appropriation by powerful forces, inimical to social work' (Ferguson, 2008, p 135).

Social work and theories of power

It will be instructive now briefly to review the ways in which power has been conceptualised by social work theorists, and to consider from which direction the emphasis on empowerment has arisen.

If we first of all consider the client-centred approach, it is the individual service user who is the focus, and whom social workers are aiming to empower. This is achieved through the development of a close enabling relationship and by conveying a sense of unconditional acceptance, by understanding and validating service users' view of the world. Little, if any, consideration is paid in this approach, however, to the societal context of service users' lives and to the notion of power residing in institutions, which could affect and compromise individuals' ability to make life changes. Conversely, the radical school of thought emphasised the structural basis of power, identifying, for example, poverty and homelessness as the sources of oppression of individual service users, who were not themselves viewed as susceptible to empowerment on an individual basis. Rather, society had first to change before individuals could benefit. The feminist school placed a welcome emphasis on the experience of women, who until then had been a marginalised group whose voices were largely unheard. Their pivotal role in family life was now highlighted, and the importance of personal relationships and female experience recognised. However, it could be argued that, in seeking to empower women as a group and bring them in from the sidelines, feminist social work over-emphasised their similarities at the expense of their individual experience. Indeed, it was this that eventually contributed to the fragmentation of this approach.

Empowerment, as conceptualised by both the radical and the feminist schools, is therefore open to criticism on grounds of its reductionist approach: the over-simplification inherent in assuming that objective characteristics, such as poverty and disability on the one hand, or being a woman on the other, have an equal impact on all those in these situations. In making this assumption, individual experience is thus minimised or discounted and hence, the potential of individuals to bring about change is underplayed or denied. The client-centred approach on the other hand, from its person–centred perspective, arguably ignores structural issues and how these can bear down on individuals and render them powerless.

In the context of social work theory, it is arguably the interactionist school which, in highlighting the *meaning* that behaviour holds for the individual, has most to offer here. By focusing on the way the individual service user interprets her world, and by using these means to understand her and afford her subjective status in her own life, she is effectively becoming more effective and powerful and able to assume more responsibility for her own life and how she chooses to behave within it. Even this approach, however, focusing as it does on individual meaning and experience, arguably fails sufficiently to emphasise the structural nature of power and to acknowledge the potential of the individual to have an impact on this.

In order to move on, it may be helpful to turn to those theorists who have written specifically about power and see how they can inform our thinking.

In mediaeval times, power was seen as 'natural and predetermined' (R. Smith, 2008, p 18) and its social existence and significance only began to be recognised in the seventeenth century by authors such as Hobbes, who recognised that it could be possessed by those individuals who held particular status within society. Hobbes was, for example, probably the first political commentator to articulate the need for strong central government, legitimated through a 'social contract,' which, he argued, would safeguard society against the possibility of chaos, or the war of 'all against all' (Hobbes, 1998 [1651]). Hobbes, and others such as Machiavelli, who viewed power simply as a means to an end, were important in recognising the social production of power, and in recognising that what was significant was not only who possessed it, but also the processes by which it was realised (R. Smith, 2008, pp 18-19).

Lukes and power

Moving forward rapidly in time, Lukes, writing in the twentieth century, relates the exercise of power to the realisation of individual interests. He distinguishes between one-, two-, and three-dimensional levels of power, and of these, focuses most attention on three-dimensional power, which he sees as being often covert, operating not only through open conflict but also through influence. This is often so subtle as to be indiscernible to those affected, who appear themselves to take on the ideology of those who hold power. We can clearly relate this to the circumstances of those lacking power, who, as we have just described, often conceptualise it only in the way they have experienced others using it, and are unaware that things could be different. If they, in their turn, reach a position where they too are able to exercise power, they are therefore likely to do so in similar ways (Lukes, 1974). An example of this might be where an individual working for an organisation gains promotion and, in taking on the role of manager, subconsciously mimics their predecessor's style. So a woman working in a male-dominated social work department, for instance, where the management is rigid and authoritarian might, in her new role, however differently she may have behaved previously, adopt some of these same characteristics herself.

Lukes also introduces the idea of 'non-decision-making', suggesting that this is as significant a use of power as actually making decisions. In a social work context this could mean, for example, that, by delaying a decision to close a children's home and allowing it to be run down until it is in such a poor condition of repair that there is no sensible alternative, those children affected are given no choice about their future and allowed no opportunity to challenge the decision. Their lack of power and control in these circumstances is therefore reinforced. Similarly, allowing children to drift in foster care, with no positive decision made about whether their long-term future should lie in adoption or elsewhere, may effectively close down some of the options originally open, and a child may end up staying in care by default.

Additionally, Lukes introduces the idea of power being exercised unconsciously, where those in powerful positions are unaware of the significance of their actions and how others might interpret them. We have already acknowledged how social workers often fail to recognise the power they possess, tending instead to see themselves as relatively powerless. Clearly, they do indeed exercise very significant power, particularly in areas such as child protection, where they operate as agents of social control, but there are other ways in which they may be unaware of the impact of their behaviour.

An example of the exercise of 'unconscious' power

In seeking to empower young people and enable them to have more of a say about their future, social workers started to invite them into meetings to discuss their options with those professionals involved with them. In doing so, they failed in some instances to offer adequate preparation in advance. Instead, they were totally unaware of the paralysing effect such involvement could have on some young people. As one young person expressed it, 'I think that bringing kids into that room where they don't know half the people and they are scared stiff is one of the most painful experiences I have ever had' (Page and Clark, 1977, p 41).

Clearly, the way this young person experienced their involvement in the meeting was the very opposite of what was intended, and indicates the importance of understanding the meaning that our behaviour, as well as their own, holds for those with whom we work. Using our earlier example, this unconscious use of power has almost certainly also been a factor in dealing particularly in the past with those who are dying, when medical and other staff have, in the perceived interests of their patients and with the best of intentions, made decisions about how, where and even when they should die.

To summarise where we have reached so far, power can therefore be perceived, as for example by the radical school in social work, almost exclusively in structuralist terms, as residing predominantly in societal institutions, where it is generally portrayed as a negative, coercive force over individuals. Or, within social work, by the client–centred approach, it can be seen more as an individual characteristic, as a potential for action, waiting to be harnessed.

Foucault and Giddens

More recent thinking has taken these ideas further and it will be helpful here briefly to revisit some of the ideas addressed earlier. Foucault, first, suggested that power was not in fact an entity that could be possessed (Foucault, 1975), but was rather something that existed independently, 'out there' so to speak, that could be exercised and claimed by anyone. He went on, moreover, to argue that power was not in itself good or bad but effectively neutral: value judgements should be reserved instead for the uses it was put to by individuals or organisations. Giddens, in the development of his structuration theory, went on to make the important suggestion that structure and agency were mutually dependent, that individuals, through their actions, shape the institutions that govern them, organisations, moreover, that should not be seen always in negative terms, but which can be either enabling or constraining. Through their transformative capacity, individuals can use their agency to influence the world around them; they can, in other words, exercise their own degree of power for good or ill. The power or agency exercised by those who are dying is a perhaps surprising example of this transformative capacity in action (Giddens, 1979).

It is power in this sense of agency that is arguably most helpful: power that, as individuals, we can choose either to claim or ignore, power that is process as well as outcome, that is interactive, rather than just an oppressive external force, that is not a commodity but an elusive entity, created out of society, which does not distinguish between the powerful and the powerless but which is 'both/and' rather than 'either/or', and which, when used positively, has the potential for each of us to engage with our environment and background and seek to transform it. So, instead of the idea of empowerment as something done to us by others, imposed, on their terms, by 'subjects' on 'objects', where people are categorised into groups dependent on their perceived objective characteristics, power becomes something that individuals claim on their own terms, and exercise in ways that are meaningful to them. In other words, it is, essentially, our belief in our own agency that empowers us and enables us to move forward, that enables us to realise our strengths and achieve our own goals.

Power and social work

We considered earlier how social workers might adopt particular methods to enhance the agency of individual service users. In this chapter, we will be focusing instead on what could perhaps be termed meta-approaches to the work: the processes through which service users are engaged at a structural level, by organisations, agencies and departments. So, in this section we will be exploring the significance of participation and consultation, and of service-user involvement. We will also explore notions of capacity-building, reflexivity, co-production and citizenship and, finally, of 'the other' and resistance.

Participation

Before moving on to explore how service users might usefully participate in the development and delivery of services, it might be helpful to consider here what we mean by participation. It has been suggested that 'a precondition for a personally meaningful participation is a sense of recognition...the space to be a subject – the "source" rather than the "object" of understanding' (C. Smith, 2000, p 72, cited in Froggett, 2002, p 143). Put differently, this suggests that those involved in promoting participation need to recognise those who will be involved as agents, people who are, by definition, capable of making choices, and worthy of respect. True participation can never in these terms therefore be merely tokenistic.

Sherry Arnstein, writing in 1969, produced a typological 'ladder of participation' (Arnstein, 1969) that has provided a common reference point ever since and been adapted for use with different groups and in varying situations. It is, for example, frequently applied in relation to work with children and young people. The 'ladder' refers to eight different levels of participation, ranging from manipulation and therapy at the lowest, non-participative level, right through to partnership, delegated power and citizen control at the highest level. In the context of the ladder, consultation is in fact, recognised as mere tokenism. In each situation it is important then, in considering how service users can have a voice, either individually or collectively, to consider what exactly we mean (and want) by participation, and whether we are, indeed, genuinely viewing participants as 'subjects' and the source, not the 'object' of understanding. It may be, for example, that children who are being introduced to the idea of sharing in decision-making, might only be ready to be 'consulted and informed', because of their age or experience.

An example of participative practice

A community organisation, providing play opportunities for local children, initially chooses simply to consult with them and inform them of what will be on offer before they start to deliver services. This is simply, however, the level at which they are initially engaged, with them moving on, as part of a continuing process, to assume some real power.

At a later date, for example, they are equally represented on an interviewing panel for new staff, where they participate as real partners and their views carry equal weight to those of the adults involved. In addition, they start to initiate bids to the Big Lottery for the funding of activities that they have themselves chosen.

It is important to recognise that 'increasing children and young people's participation in an organisation is a political process about shifting power relationships' (Kirby et al, 2003, cited by SCIE, 2009) and is, in our terms, enhancing their agency.

Service user involvement

This level of involvement in an organisation is also an example of service user involvement. This can arguably be traced back to 1970, when a seminal work, *The client speaks* (Mayer and Timms, 1970) was published. This book represented the first significant attempt in social work to access the views of those receiving services and identify what they saw as helpful or otherwise in a social worker and some of the findings proved challenging. Some 'clients' identified, for example, that they felt social workers were trying to 'catch them out' (p 124) while the emphasis on their individual feelings was seen as irrelevant and insensitive, especially when their economic circumstances were such that they were often struggling just to survive. The implications of these views for an analysis of power relationships in the profession are no doubt clear: social workers were perceived as potentially abusing their own power and failing to understand the realities of their clients' lives; while the absence of any sense of power felt by clients themselves was reinforced by neglecting the impact of structural issues on their lives.

Soon after this very influential publication appeared in social work libraries, the rights movement, which started in the United States, but rapidly spread to the UK, emphasised the entitlement of groups of individuals to societal recognition and services that addressed their needs, as they experienced them. In broad social terms, it was the civil rights and women's liberation movements of the 1960s and 1970s that were most significant and which particularly attracted media publicity and led ultimately to changes in legislation. In the social work context, however, it was an altogether quieter revolution that was under way.

In the wake of the feminist movement, other groups now began to find their own voice, to speak out and let others know how they really experienced life, to identify what was important to them and which issues they wished to see addressed. They began, in other words, to experience and find expression for their own emerging sense of agency.

This movement, in the social work context, arguably began when mental health service users started to self-advocate, to speak out for themselves and others in similar situations, and to throw light on their experiences. A key figure in this process was Peter Beresford, (e.g. Beresford et al, 2007). An ex-user of mental health services himself, Beresford remains a powerful exponent of service-user involvement. He has, for example, helped to develop a new type of 'user-controlled' research, through which those with disabilities identify the questions to which they want answers, and 'challenge knowledge based on traditional assumptions of validity' (Benjamin, 2005). To quote Beresford directly, 'What people like me are interested in, and can demonstrate, is that those who have been seen as the problem maybe have some very, very helpful things to offer in terms of developing the solution' (Benjamin, 2005). And, as Ferguson suggests, following on from the ideas of Williams and Popay, it is important that 'research...considers...what both the system and the welfare subject contribute to the meanings and outcomes of interventions' and considers 'what the welfare subject her- or himself brings to these dynamic relationships and a more subtle analysis of the interface between subject and system' (Ferguson, 2003, p 209).

The service-user movement may have started with mental health users, but it has gone on to encompass a wide range of other traditional users of social work services. These include, for example, vulnerable older people, those with learning disabilities and children in care. Indeed, the combined interests of all service user organisations are now represented by the organisation Shaping Our Lives of which Beresford is Chair.

Who cares?

One example of the success of the service-user movement was the founding of the *Who cares?* magazine, initiated in 1985, which was set up by young people in the care system, and led to the formation, in 1992, of the organisation of the same name. This gives young people who are 'looked after' a platform 'to relay their concerns and views to decision-makers in local and central government' (www.thewhocarestrust.org.uk). Through these means, this organisation and its counterpart, A National Voice, run by and for young people who are in or leaving care, have also contributed to changes in legislation, to, for example, the Children

(Leaving Care) Act 2000 and to Every Child Matters 2004 (DfES, 2004). In addition, young people and individual service users generally are now starting to be seen, in this context, as 'experts in their own lives' (Postle and Beresford, 2007). Moreover, the newly-acquired skills and confidence associated with self-help and campaigning activities, results in more general capacity-building. Of equal importance to these national changes therefore, has been the impact on individual young people, of their membership of Who Cares? or of A National Voice, with young people realising their own abilities, learning to value themselves, and going on to achieve success in other areas of their lives.

The influence of service users continues to grow and to expand into new and perhaps unlikely areas. A recent article focuses on user engagement of offenders. As Mark Johnson, a rehabilitated offender and former drug user himself eloquently explains,

> We believe that only offenders – that is, users of the criminal justice system – can reduce offending...now they are being handed some personal responsibility... .Prison councils...will offer a channel for the hidden people at society's extremities to articulate how they can help, and be helped, to change. Most of all, run peer-to-peer, they are a model of engagement. (Johnson, 2009)

Collective agency

The service user movement provides a powerful example of the transformative potential or capacity of individual or, in this instance, collective agency. As Ferguson identifies, 'A space has opened up which provides greater autonomy for welfare subjects to define their identities while interacting in new ways with "expert systems", including social services and other "helping" agencies' (Ferguson, 2003, p 201). For, as has been suggested, not only are individuals able, perhaps for the first time, to experience themselves as subjects of their own lives; the very context in which they live, the structures that have an impact on them, and the way they are perceived by society can all begin to be transformed. As Barnes recognised, 'The significance of user movements...goes beyond what they are able to achieve to benefit those whose identities and interests are represented directly by such groups, to their potential to act as transformative agents, altering the perspective of dominant groups' (Barnes, 1997, p 71, cited in Ferguson, 2008, p 81). What is also important, as Oliver has observed (Oliver, 2004) is that the emphasis is on people doing things for themselves, not being 'done to' by professionals. The role of social workers is therefore, in this context, 'to give support and work alongside people' respecting the agendas that they choose to set rather than seeking to impose our own' (Postle and Beresford, 2007, p 155).

Reflexivity

Theoretically linked with service-user movements is the idea of reflexive monitoring, or the ability to reflect on our behaviour, which both distinguishes humans from animals and acknowledges that our actions are intentional (Giddens, 1979). It is, after all, through reflecting on their circumstances, that service users become engaged in the sorts of movements we have just described. Intentionality is not, however, something that can be assumed in all behaviour and this is an area to which we will return.

Taking this idea further for the moment, however, Giddens moved on to develop the notion of the 'reflexive project of the self' (Giddens, 1991). He suggests that modern life tends to impoverish individual action, but believes that 'human beings can react against social circumstances which they find oppressive...and engage boldly with the outer social world' (Giddens, 1991, p 175). The focus here is on what individuals choose to do once they have a degree of autonomy. As he puts it, 'The reflexive project of the self...consists in the sustaining of coherent, yet continuously revised, biographical narratives' and 'takes place in the context of multiple choice.' It 'generates programmes of actualisation and mastery' (Giddens, 1991, p 9). We are all now, in the context of modern society, and partly as a result of more effective communications systems, the internet and the media, far more knowledgeable about how the world operates, and potentially more able, in these circumstances to shape our lives in the ways we want. Bratman expresses it in this way: 'We are planning agents; our agency extends over time and sometimes at least, we govern our own actions' (Bratman, 2007, p 3).

The use of narrative

So where does the idea of reflexivity belong in a social work context? Giddens links reflexivity with the notion of 'life-planning', whereby, through the creation of personal narratives, which we discussed in the previous chapter, individuals make sense of themselves, their history and their current circumstances, and plan for their futures. We noted earlier how important are a sense of coherence and identity; that they are crucial components of positive mental and physical health. Those who are users of social work services, however, are likely not to be skilled in planning their lives. If, however, services are developed that help them to forge a 'narrative identity' (Sands, 1996, p 169, cited in Fook, 2002, p 75), those who are service users might be enabled to de- and reconstruct their own identities to integrate probably adverse experiences into a coherent sense of whole.

An example of personal narration

A convicted offender has had the opportunity while in custody, of discovering an interest in and aptitude for horticulture. On release, he is offered support tailored to his individual needs, and as a result is able to secure employment in this field. He can, with help, begin to view himself as a 'gardener', rather than simply as an 'ex-con'. In doing so, he is reconstructing his identity, building on his newfound strengths, and is able to move on from the label that has previously been ascribed to him, to a new and more positive sense of himself.

An important ingredient in the idea of narrative is the notion of movement, of things moving forward. So an individual's identity can be recognised as being in a constant state of flux, the result of 'an internalised relationship between an inner reflective agent and external experiences' (Sands, 1996, p 169, in Fook, 2002, p 71). In other words, things can change and be otherwise, and in coming to believe this, fixed identities can be challenged and resisted, new meaning can emerge and a sense of agency can be restored to individuals. This is, arguably, what is happening when an individual engages in therapy, when, through the therapeutic process facilitated by the therapist, the 'patient' reflects on their life experiences and is able to reframe them and move on. Equally, in situations where individual service users are becoming aware of their own agency, they might start to link up with others in similar circumstances and together begin to have an impact on the way services are delivered to themselves and others.

Capacity-building

One way that this process is currently conceptualised, is in the term 'capacity-building', an expression that has emerged in the social work lexicon over recent years, where it is taken to mean the development of 'a greater mutual sense of power' (R. Smith, 2008, p 159). This term, in itself, suggests an ongoing process, one in which the service user is involved directly, and, as part of this experience, begins to forge a new, more powerful sense of whom they are. 'Capacity-building' also suggests a collaborative venture: something that potentially involves not just individuals, but whole communities, that brings together people in similar situations. It aims to 'strengthen the skills and abilities of people and communities enabling them to take effective action and leading roles in the development of their community' (Faith–Based Regeneration Network website, 2009). It is, in effect, a tool for community development.

So, if we, in social work, are charged with responsibility for helping to build service users' capacity, what does this mean in practice? It means that in our organisations, we need to be constantly mindful of how the users of our services can be involved in their creation and development. It means that we need to encourage them, as reflexive individuals, to reflect on their experiences as service users, and to use this, alongside us, the service providers, to inform our thinking of what is needed in the future. It means that we, as practitioners, need simultaneously, to reflect on our own practice, and learn ultimately to work, not hierarchically, in isolation from those we are seeking to support, but in collaboration with them, accepting that they are the experts in their own lives and best placed to know what will be needed for service users of the future. In practice, it means we need to develop mechanisms for hearing the voices of service users and involving them in genuine partnership in service development.

Co-production

One way in which individual capacity can be built on or enhanced is through service users engaging directly with providers in a collaborative enterprise to bring about new services. Known as co-production, this process 'challenges the dominant role of the professional and shifts the service user from the role of passive recipient to that of a valued participant' (SCIE, 2009). It also 'redefines the idea of the expert, with the users of services recognised as possessing expertise that can be shared with providers' (SCIE, 2009). It features at one level in situations where adults, as part of the personalisation agenda, help to negotiate their own individual care packages, but has the potential for wider influence when services are being designed and delivered. Here it is, as has been described, 'a potentially transformative way of thinking about partnerships, power, resources, risks and outcomes' (SCIE, 2009), involving the creation of mutual trust and respect.

An example of parent empowerment (2)

Local authority 'B' decides that, instead of consulting with parents only after their Parenting Charter has been drawn up, they should be involved at the very beginning, given the opportunity to identify what is right and wrong with existing services, and able to share in the responsibility of drafting new arrangements. In this way, not only are parents engaged in genuine power-sharing, with the associated benefits for them as individuals; they are also influential in altering the very structures that affect their lives and, as a result, potentially more committed to supporting any new services that are put in place.

One example of where co-production is already delivering is in the Expert Patients Programme Community Interest Company, a not-for-profit social enterprise, previously run by the NHS. This is where patients 'tackle the illness in partnership with their clinicians, rather than being passive recipients of care', and where the patients are recognised as potentially as 'knowledgeable as clinical professionals in the day-to-day management of their condition' (Campbell, 2009). This programme is already proving invaluable for those with long-term medical conditions such as diabetes, arthritis and heart disease, where sufferers and their carers learn how better to manage their situation. In doing so, they also regain a degree of power in a situation where they would probably otherwise have surrendered much of this to the medical profession, which is an important consideration. Potentially, they may also, through sharing their personal experience of disease, be able to influence the care and treatment of other sufferers in the future.

Direct payments

The practice of 'direct payments' offers a further example of how service users can retain some power in difficult circumstances. Under this system, implemented as a result of the Community Care Act 1996, money goes directly to disabled or vulnerable older people to purchase their own care. These people then become the employers of those who look after them, responsible for everything that this involves, including CRB checks on those caring for them. This system has been described as 'the most successful public policy in the area of social care' (Prime Minister's Strategy Unit et al, 2005), and has been recognised as making a most important contribution to the independence and well-being of people with disabilities (PSSRU, 2008).

Another recent initiative, known as Self-Directed Support, similarly aims to 'liberate service users from being cared for' by also giving them their own budgets, and 'the support and freedom to make their own decisions about where and how they live'. Simon Duffy, spokesperson of In Control, interviewed by *The Guardian* acknowledges that 'the care system creates powerlessness' (Gould, 2008) and has supported Wigan council's efforts to 'escape' those with learning difficulties from institutional care. Effectively, this approach, like those described in the previous chapter, focuses on enabling people to find their own solutions for their own lives. Interestingly, Duffy comes from a background in philosophy, and views his work as a way of shifting the moral basis of care 'towards clarity about rights and duties' (Gould, 2008).

Co-production is not without its attendant difficulties, such as the need to support both users and professionals new to the concept, together with the potential for problems in establishing accountability when plans go awry. However, these issues should not be seen as insurmountable, and the potential of co-production for enhancing individual agency and re-shaping service structures is considerable. Until now, it has been used almost exclusively in adult social and physical care and with those who have learning difficulties, but it is possible to envisage a significant role for co-production with other user groups, including young people leaving care and offenders in the prison system.

Citizenship

Steve Jones, Chief Executive of Wigan council, where Self-Directed Support is being introduced, observed that 'people with learning difficulties should be citizens, but...social services don't do citizenship' (Gould, 2008). The concept of citizenship is where arguably, people are most fully recognised as having the capacity to be self-directing and seen as having equal status. It has been suggested that citizens are now seen less as passive bearers of rights and, partly as a result of the feminist movement, more as active political agents (Lister, 1998). Citizenship, according to Lister, is both 'participation' and 'rights': participation in the sense of individuals expressing their human agency in the political arena; and rights where people are enabled to act as agents. In other words, citizenship represents the point at which the notion of rights and participation are synthesised in the concept of agency, where the individual is acting upon and potentially changing the world, which, in its turn, structures the choices open to the citizen (Lister, 1998). How service users can contribute to society, and in doing so, can enhance their own self-image is therefore central to this notion, with co-production of services providing an example of how this can be achieved in practice.

Agency and 'the other'

Society, however, contains certain groups of people who are not always fully accepted as citizens, but who tend to be socially excluded and singled out as different. It may be helpful here to consider the processes by which societies and cultures exclude those whom they want to subordinate or who do not fit into their society.

Edward Said

A Palestinian refugee who escaped to Cairo as a teenager, and later settled in the USA, Edward Said took as his subject the idea of 'Orientalism'. By this, put simply, he meant the classification of the East as something different from the Western world that we inhabit. As he expressed it, 'We ("the powerful") become more rational, virtuous, mature, "normal" because "the Oriental", (or Other) is irrational, depraved (fallen), childlike, "different"' (Said, 1978, p 40). In other words, Said argued, by creating an idea of Orientalism, we define ourselves and our culture as the norm and as relatively powerful in relation to 'the other', who are viewed, by contrast, as strange, as an 'object' of study. As Malek, quoted in Said (1978, p 97), put it, 'this "object" of study will be...passive, non-participating... above all, non-active, non-autonomous' (Malek, 1963).

Moreover, in seeing Oriental people merely as objects of study, 'they were rarely seen or looked at; they were seen through, analysed not as citizens, or even people but as problems to be solved' (Said, 1978, p 207). In their 'otherness', Oriental people were, in other words, denied a sense of their own humanity, of being people themselves, with their own valid ways of interpreting and being in the world. In this way, the interests of the West were prioritised and promoted: it was their world view that held sway, their economic and political ends that were served. The Orient, in its otherness, did not feature.

In an afterword to *Orientalism*, written in 1994, Said, reflecting on his earlier work, made the following observation: 'Each age and society recreates its "Others". Far from a static thing...identity of self or of "other" is a much worked-over historical, social, intellectual, and political process that takes place as a contest involving individuals and institutions in all societies' (Said, 1994, p 35). He referred to the existence, in today's world, of a variety of 'others', including, for example, outsiders and refugees, noting the implications for the sense of identity of those individuals in these groups; and for the distribution of power in society.

Taking a historical example, it is possible, to recognise the idea of 'the other' in the writings of Stedman-Jones (1971) and Thompson (1978) both of whom identified the ways in which working people were treated as different and 'other' during the industrialisation of the nineteenth century, and who have attempted to bring them in from the margins. Indeed, Thompson viewed his own work partly as an attempt to rescue working people from 'the enormous condescension of posterity' (Thompson, 1963, p 13). Stedman-Jones also, for example, notes how poor people were seen as a 'problem', as an undifferentiated mass. They were not seen as individual people but rather as a collective threat that had to be controlled. They were viewed as the 'residuum', as essentially different from the controlling classes, as 'the other' (Stedman-Jones, 1971).

In a similar vein, current attitudes towards crime and those who commit it have been highlighted in the work of Garland (Garland, 2001). In this book, he charts the decline in welfarist approaches over the last thirty years, the re-emergence of punitive measures and a change in the emotional tone of penal policy, which no longer refers to 'decency', 'humanity' and compassion, but rather to fear of crime, and the protection of society. The victim, he suggests, has become Everyman, and by implication the offender has been cast in the role of 'the other'.

The idea of 'the other' can, as Said suggested, also be clearly recognised today in our treatment of other groups. These might include, for example, those suffering from mental illness, black people, or refugees and asylum-seekers. These groups, seen through the eyes of more dominant groups, might be viewed as posing a threat, either to their physical safety, their children's well-being or their economic livelihood. They are viewed as 'not like us', as outsiders, not belonging. As Dominelli explained 'The "self" exists because there is an "other" to whom one can compare oneself.' This enables 'the "self" to externalise the "other", and facilitates the act of viewing the "other" in an antagonistic and hierarchical relationship to oneself' (Dominelli, 2004, p 76, cited in R. Smith, 2008, p 43).

In his work, Said draws out and makes explicit the idea of binary thinking, the way of viewing the world that divides its citizens into two groups: into 'us' and 'them,' young and old, haves and have-nots, the socially included and the excluded – and into teachers and taught, into social workers and service users. In addition, his writing represents the gradual shift, in Western thought, away from the 'grand narratives' of the Enlightenment era, and offers a new way of interpreting the world and the experience of those who inhabit it. As one of the early 'post-modernists', he seeks rather to recognise and honour different ways of being and of seeing, to bring out into the open the means by which we objectify 'others', particularly those of different cultures, and in doing so, deny their sense of identity and invalidate their experiences.

This process of 'othering' is emphasised in politics and by the media. The notion of an underclass, of the 'socially excluded' is, at one and the same time, both a way of identifying those outside the mainstream of society and in need of support, leading to new policies aimed at their inclusion; but also a means of labelling them, of keeping them in their place, of reinforcing their outsider status and conversely emphasising the feeling of 'normality' that the rest of society can enjoy. For those identified as 'the other', they are effectively blamed for being the victims of their own oppression. They are seen as the embodiment of the problems they face, and not as individuals with difficulties that can be overcome.

There have been occasional attempts to redress this tendency, however, which deserve recognition. One of these was the report entitled *People like us*, focusing on safeguards for children living away from home (Utting, 1998). In this publication, Utting endeavoured to emphasise the shared humanity of young people in the 'looked after' system, and their right to be treated and to expect to be treated with respect, just like other young people who were fortunate enough still to be living at home. Other examples here might include Lord Justice Butler-Sloss' declaration, in the context of the Cleveland Enquiry into child sexual abuse, that 'a child is a person, not an object of concern' (Butler-Sloss, 1988); and the introduction, already noted, of direct payments, where those adults assessed as needing help from social services, receive money to arrange their own care, and by these means, retain the capacity to define their own agenda, rather than having this interpreted by others.

'The other' and agency

For our present purposes, the practice of 'othering' is the antithesis of what a sense of agency can offer. By marginalising particular groups in society, we are, in effect, denying them any sense of agency and reducing them, as discussed earlier, to objective rather than subjective status in their own lives. Those seen as 'the other' are the people most likely to be users of the services we provide, those who, either for structural reasons such as poverty, homelessness or ethnicity are excluded from the mainstream of society; or whose behaviour, as offenders or through mental illness or incapacity, marks them out as different. It is these people who are not viewed as 'people like us', who are the 'socially excluded' and categorised as falling outside the norm and who, arguably, most need to resist these labels and begin to experience a sense of their own agency.

Resistance is a key concept here. It is after all what happens when people who are labelled in ways that neither respect their differences nor their rights as individuals, react against the negative labels ascribed to them by dominant groups, and start to assert their own meanings and truth. It is what was happening, for example, when the 'gay pride' movement was launched, when gay and lesbian people came together to affirm their own sense of strength and identity (R. Smith, 2008); and it was present, too, in the 'women reclaim the night' marches of the 1980s, when women asserted their right to be out of doors safely at night, at a time when the Yorkshire Ripper was still at large. So resistance is about relationships, a 'strategy... to negate and redefine prior assumptions about...needs, status or behaviour' (R. Smith, 2008, p 136).

The arts and resistance

One way in which those defined as 'the other' have resisted this label has been through the use of culture and the arts. We can see this in a variety of forms: from visual art and photography, to poetry and novels, and perhaps most powerfully, in theatre. Sir Richard Eyre, Director of the National Theatre for ten years in the 1980s and 1990s, made out a powerful case for theatre in these terms:

> If we have to look for a political justification for the arts we might argue that the arts enable us to put ourselves in the minds, eyes, ears and hearts of other human beings, and hence equip us to understand people who are different from ourselves in gender or class or race or religion – or simply that they're not us. ...The arts add to the sum of human understanding. (Eyre, 2005)

The potential of the arts: an example

Lee Hall's play, *The pitmen painters*, was originally produced at the National Theatre and then shown around the country. The play tells the story of how, in the 1930s, Northumbrian miners received art appreciation classes through the Workers' Educational Association, and revealed that they possessed extraordinary talent, with their paintings going on to be displayed in galleries throughout the UK. Bunting, reviewing the play, writes of its themes of 'autonomy, engagement and empowerment' while Hall himself speaks of wanting 'above all to remind people of what the working class is capable of: that given the right circumstances ordinary people achieve extraordinary things. They can be much more than passive consumers of a culture they are rarely allowed to create' (Bunting, 2008a). Most movingly, one of the painters themselves said:

> When I paint as we do in our group I have a feeling of freedom. There is a feeling of being my own boss for a change. When I have done a piece of painting I feel that something has happened, not only to the panel or canvas but to myself. For a time, I have enjoyed a sense of mastery – of having made something real. (Wilson, cited in Feaver, 2009)

So what do examples such as this tell us? How can they inform our thinking and inspire our work? What is happening, it could be suggested, in *The pitmen painters* is effectively that the people concerned are moving from being objects in their own lives to becoming subjects; they are beginning to resist the labels, the 'othering' that has previously deprived them of a voice, and are learning to speak for themselves. And in so doing, they are not only discovering their own sense of agency, but, what is equally important, they are challenging and changing the way that they are viewed by the rest of society.

Conclusion

In this chapter, we opened with a consideration of dying and how, perhaps surprisingly, even at this late stage in life, individuals have the potential to express themselves and their needs, to act agentically and influence the manner in which they die and, indeed, the way in which death is managed. We went on to explore the notion of empowerment and considered why agency is, for our purposes, a more helpful term; and then moved on to consider the ways in which power, at a management or departmental level, can be shared, with service users variously participating in service delivery, and, through user involvement, capacity building, co-production and citizenship, contributing their own valuable perspective and influencing how services are developed and delivered.

Finally, we looked at the concept of 'the other', how it originated and the way it is used to exclude those whom society views as different or threatening. We noted however that the kind of labelling that this 'othering' involves can be challenged and resisted, particularly through different art forms, with the opportunity that these provide for redefining the status quo and helping us to see things differently.

In the next chapter we will continue to explore the notion of agency in relation to resistance, this time in a political context. In doing so, we will shift our focus abroad, to Africa, South America and India where we will be examining the work and writings of Frantz Fanon, Paolo Freire and Amartya Sen. Taking these geographical areas by way of example, we will consider agency theory in the light of some of the issues that concern developing countries and whether or not their experience has anything relevant to contribute.

FOUR

Agency and structure: individuals in society

It is possible for human beings to become agentically effective...in evaluating their social context, creatively envisioning alternatives and collaborating with others to bring about its transformation. (Margaret Archer, 2000, p 308)

All organisms bequeath to their successors when they die a slightly changed environment...we make our own history, though not in circumstances of our own choosing. (Rose et al, 1984, p 13)

Introduction

So far, we have explored the concept of agency from a purely British standpoint. We have used it as the lens through which to consider social work activity in our own culture, to explore how we, as professionals, might most effectively engage with service users and how they, in turn, can, in the right circumstances, assume some responsibility and control for the services they use and help to shape them. We have seen how agency can be a helpful concept in this context, a means of identifying effective approaches and methods, which build on and enhance both our own and service users' self-belief and efficacy.

We are now going to develop a more internationalist perspective. In the first part of this chapter we will be exploring the ideas of Frantz Fanon and Paolo Freire, influential thinkers who have written about their work and experiences in colonial North Africa and in Latin America; and will move on to consider the writing of Amartya Sen, and his analysis, from a contrasting economic viewpoint, of how ideas of freedom and agency can have an impact on economic development. We will then reflect on the relevance of these authors' ideas to our own concerns, to our education and social welfare practices and to our own British culture and experience.

In conclusion, we will start to consider the essentially political nature of social work and will argue that, particularly perhaps in the current climate of standardisation and centrally prescribed targets, it cannot be undertaken effectively without some level of political engagement.

The work of Fanon, Freire and Sen

Fanon

In *The wretched of the earth*, Frantz Fanon took as his subject the Algerian war of independence, the struggle of Algerian 'natives' to free themselves from colonial rule. His book concerned, in his terms, the 'crime' of colonisation'. Fanon was writing from an interesting perspective. A black psychiatrist, he was born in the Caribbean, in Martinique, but educated in France, a background that perhaps offered him a unique insight into the Algerian situation. Fanon characterised the effect of colonialisation as one where 'the indigenous population is discerned only as an indistinct mass' and where 'the governing race is first and foremost those who come from elsewhere, those who are unlike the original inhabitants, "the others"' (Fanon, 1965, p 39). Moreover, he argued, colonialism imposes a dichotomy on those it subjugates, with individuals living in 'a motionless, Manichaistic world, a world of statues' (p 51). They are not living, breathing, creative human beings, but 'petrified', as if cast in stone, and by implication, unable to act on their own behalf to shape their circumstances.

In this way, Fanon, who could perhaps identify to some extent with those on both sides of this dichotomy, was able to interpret and express the psychological damage inflicted on whole populations by colonialisation. He was able to give voice to the 'psychical invasion' that those subjected to racism experience (Hoggett, 2001). He described their hitherto unarticulated feelings of rage and frustration, and suggested that they needed to find common cause with each other, to achieve community cohesion and take united action against their oppressors. In doing so, he demonstrated that, in his own words, 'mastery of language affords remarkable power' (Fanon, 1952, p 17). Ultimately, however, he believed that it was only through violence that 'the "thing" which has been colonised becomes man' (Fanon, 1965, pp 35–6) and through which his self-respect could be restored.

Despite, or perhaps because of his explicit advocacy of violence, Fanon's work proved hugely influential in anti-colonialist movements throughout the world, and was also of great significance in black consciousness-raising. His work continues, however, as I will argue later on in this chapter, to be significant today.

Freire

Paolo Freire's major work, *The pedagogy of the oppressed*, was written a few years later (Freire, 1970). A Brazilian by birth, Freire too, had an interesting background, being imprisoned and then exiled in the 1960s. As a Catholic, he subsequently became advisor on education to the World Council of Churches, and later, under Allende's rule, to Chile. Like Fanon, Freire's focus was on those denied a voice, in his case those in Brazil who were poor or oppressed. In his writing, Freire referred to 'the culture of silence' of the dispossessed, who largely as a result of the system of education to which they were subjected, were kept, he argued, in a state of ignorance and lethargy. Through their social positioning within existing social, economic and political structures, and as victims of 'the false generosity of paternalism', they learned to fear freedom, to internalise their own oppression and become complicit in it. Or, as a more recent writer describes it, they were 'constructive in' their 'own dependency and powerlessness' (Hoggett, 2001, p 43).

This, however, was not, according to Freire, their vocation. On the contrary, an individual's natural calling 'is to be a Subject who acts upon and transforms his world...which is not a static and closed order, a given reality which man must accept and to which he must adjust' but 'a problem to be worked on and solved. It is the material used by man to create liberty' (Freire, 1970, p 32). As such, the world is therefore in a constant state of flux. It is not a fixed entity which can be 'sorted' once and for all, but something that possesses its own dynamic, that needs to be constantly subject to critical analysis and continually transformed (Freire, 1970). And for those subject to oppression to be able to reach the position where they can influence the world in this way, required, he suggested, a new kind of teaching, one which the oppressed themselves helped to develop, which 'has to be forged *with*, not *for* the oppressed' (Freire, p 33). What was required was, in essence, a democratisation of education. For man to become free, he needed to be able to reflect on his oppression, to realise that his situation was not immutable, but one which he could himself act upon and transform. In Freire's terms, this was the *praxis*, and the *self*-belief that underpinned this was, according to Freire, while not sufficient in itself, a necessary condition for this to occur.

For Freire this self-belief, a sense that individuals held within themselves the potential and the ability to shape their world, was absolutely fundamental. Talking to local people about how they could personally act on their situation, he was met with the typical response: 'What can I do, I'm only a peasant', and it was this hopeless, fatalistic attitude that Freire was at pains to challenge. He believed, moreover, that 'while no-one liberates himself by his own efforts alone, neither is he liberated by others' (Freire, p 53). In other words, in our own terms, people could not 'be empowered'; their liberation could only be achieved through dialogue with others, the oppressors.

Dialogue was, in Friere's view, key. He believed that everyone, through discussion with others, was able to engage critically with the world, to give it meaning, and through doing so, to reach an understanding of how society could be changed. Indeed, it was only through communication and dialogue that meaning could be found. As he stated, 'Dialogue is the encounter between man, mediated by the world, in order to name the world' (Freire, p 76).

For Freire, it was education that provided the means for this dialogue to take place. Traditionally, he argued, education was merely a process of 'depositing' information as a 'gift', from those in power to those without it. Its content was therefore pre-determined and not open to question. If education was seen in dialogical terms, however, it became a different thing altogether. In Freire's words, 'knowledge emerges only through invention and reinvention, through the restless, impatient, continuing, hopeful enquiry human beings pursue in the world, with the world, and with each other' (Freire, p 348). Education became, in other words, something that was co-produced, where the knowledge and understanding of those on the receiving end, was seen as having as much value as that of the educators; where those being educated as well as those delivering it, could be seen as participating subjects, and not as objects. We will return to the significance of Freire's view of the purpose of education later on in this chapter.

Both Fanon and Freire believed in a world that was essentially open to change, whose features were not permanent and immutable, but open to transformation by individuals and groups who believed they had the power to transform society. Neither author subscribed to the idea of a 'well-behaved present, nor a pre-determined future' (Freire, p 65); their views were rather, in our current terminology, anti-deterministic, subscribing instead to a vision that allowed for individual agency and expression, to a present and a future that were open and had the potential for change.

Sen

Amartya Sen, who has lived in India, Britain and the USA, writes, as a Nobel prize-winning economist, from a very different starting-point. Author of a number of influential books, he incorporates into his work a profound sense of humanity. His is not the dry academic writing of a university-bound economist, but the work of someone who is truly engaged with the world and its problems, and who, using his own multicultural background, draws on a wide breadth of personal experience to illuminate his arguments.

In *Development as freedom* (Sen, 1999a) Sen takes as his subject the worldwide incidence of deprivation, destitution and oppression, focusing particularly on the developing areas of Asia, such as Bangladesh. He argues that education, particularly of women, is fundamental to reducing fertility rates, to improving health and to greater longevity. As an example, he quotes the case of Kerala, in South India, where the education of girls has resulted in higher levels of literacy, smaller families and enhanced rates of child survival. Education, in other words, not only serves the interests of the women concerned, through employment and other opportunities, but also the lives of their children and society as a whole. In Sen's view, education brings freedom – a freedom that is 'both the primary end and...the principle means of development' (Sen, 1999a, p xii). Freedom not only leads to better outcomes, but the process of exercising it, in itself enhances individual well-being.

By freedom, Sen is referring to agency – to individuals finding their own voice and using it to exercise choice, to act on their circumstances and initiate change. He argues that 'a freedom-centred understanding of economics and of the process of development is very much an agent-oriented view. With adequate social opportunities, individuals can effectively shape their own destiny and help each other' (Sen, 1999a, p W11). For Sen, agency and well-being go hand in hand. Where people, through education and employment, are freed from destitution and poverty, they experience a sense of freedom that is fundamental to individual agency, and their self-confidence, as well as their physical and emotional health improves. A welfare approach that fails to recognise the potential of service users, that views them merely as 'passive recipients of dispersed benefits' and hand-outs, denies them the opportunity to act as 'the dynamic promoters of social transformation' (Sen, 1999a, p 11).

Moreover, Sen recognises the dynamic interplay between agency and social structure. As he puts it:

> There is a deep complementarity between individual agency and social arrangements. It is important to give simultaneous recognition to the centrality of individual freedom *and* to the force of social influences on the extent and reach of individual freedom. To counter the problems that we face, we have to see individual freedom as a social commitment. (Sen, 1999a, p 12)

In other words, by recognising the two-way relationship between structure and agency, not only is individual well-being enhanced, but social arrangements are made more effective and appropriate.

Sen argues, not for revolution, but for a gradualist, developmental approach, where economics and social and political activities work hand in hand. His is an approach that is also essentially anti-determinist, because, as he recognises, change does take place. For him, change is multi-faceted, with different kinds of freedom complementing and building on each other. In this context, partnership between relevant agencies is key. Perhaps, above all, however, Sen recognises the crucial nature of education, whose potential for unlocking individual agency, and the choices and responsibilities associated with this, is fundamental.

So what do these different perspectives have to contribute to our own agenda? What light can these authors and their ideas, relating as they largely do to cultures that are very different from our own, throw on our work and the circumstances of those with whom we engage, in our own society? In the next section we will be exploring their relevance not only to social work in Britain today, but also, in the first instance, to education.

Education and social work

Central to the writing and work of both Freire and Sen is a belief in the power of education to act as a transformative force in achieving change, not just in the lives of individuals but in society as a whole. For Freire, this was achieved through dialogue between teacher and learner, providing the means through which learners' views and experiences could be taken seriously. Education should not merely privilege existing knowledge but should recognise that what pupils themselves brought to the encounter was equally valid. The knowledge residing in those who were oppressed was perhaps masked by their circumstances, but it was nevertheless immanent, he believed, in all people, of whatever status and background. Sen, on the other hand, perceived education as an essential prerequisite to the acquisition of freedom or agency, the means by which people, particularly women and subsequently their children, could achieve more status and power in society, and through which standards of health and social care could be raised, and development, on a societal scale, be achieved.

The relevance of this thinking for our own society is no doubt clear. In Britain, our education system is currently predicated on children progressing through the national curriculum, receiving a more-or-less standardised input from their teachers and achieving results: results which are measured and assessed through standard assessments or SATS, and via league tables, against which schools, teachers and children themselves are evaluated. Education, in other words, is something whose content is almost entirely determined by those in charge, and whose success is measured simply by the end product or outcome. It is, in Freire's terms, information that is deposited into pupils or students, as a gift by those in power, who control the agenda.

Education and prevention

There are other ways of viewing education, however, even in our own society. Dyson, in a paper on 'The role of education in prevention' recognises its potential as 'a mediating factor between the patterns of advantage and disadvantage in learners' backgrounds and their life-chances' (Dyson, 2004). He suggests that children bring into school 'different sets of resources' which can 'interact with what the school offers and expects' (Dyson, 2004). He recognises that what children achieve in terms of educational outcomes and ultimately life chances, is 'determined neither by their backgrounds nor by the actions of the education system, but by a complex interaction between the two' (Dyson, 2004). In Dyson's terms, education is potentially not, therefore, merely something that is 'deposited' as a 'gift' into pupil children and young people, but rather a dynamic encounter between educator and learner, one to which both bring something of equal value and from which each can benefit and learn.

This analysis of what education can and, in Dyson's view, should offer, is of particular relevance, he believes, in considering the position of children with special needs, or those who come from disadvantaged or deprived backgrounds. For the most part, our education system subscribes to a deficit model in relation to these children. They are seen as lacking in certain aspects or attributes, compared with the norm; they do not behave in the same way as other, more advantaged children, they do not respond in the same ways and they often embarrass us. They are, in essence, 'other', and not like us. As Said would argue, in viewing them in these terms, they serve to emphasise and enhance our own sense of worth, of normality and superiority, and our associated feelings of power, relative to these others.

Like the colonial 'natives' that Fanon described in Algeria, and Freire's Brazilians, these children are likely to internalise this view of themselves. Instead of recognising their own strengths, their potential in terms of what they might achieve, they are more likely to compare themselves adversely with those children who are from more privileged backgrounds, who are more academically able, more likely ultimately to achieve status and power in society. They recognise their increasing exclusion from mainstream society – and not surprisingly they resent it. As time goes on, this internalised negative self-image often starts to express itself in anti-social and criminal behaviour, as the young people concerned live down to the expectations that they and others have of them. They are becoming the next generation of the 'socially excluded', and are themselves complicit in this progression.

Education as an encounter

However, as Freire in particular has emphasised, education can also be a powerful force in the opposite direction. If it were conceptualised differently, viewed more as an encounter between teacher and pupil, a dialogue to which each was able to contribute on more equal terms, with their contribution legitimised and valued, these same children might start to feel differently about themselves. They might develop a greater feeling of self worth, and, in our terms, begin to experience a sense of agency, a belief that they too had something to contribute to society. They might be able to resist the labels that are imposed on them, and through reflecting on their circumstances, achieve personal successes which, in turn, were meaningful to society as a whole.

Some examples of imaginative forms of education

These sentiments and aspirations are, of course, not new, but echo much of the thinking that already goes on in schools and colleges up and down the country, particularly among teachers and educators who feel constrained by the current education system. Indeed, despite these constraints, numerous examples of innovative and inspiring ways of working do exist, particularly perhaps in the voluntary and community sector, where there is more freedom to break new ground. One example here is the work of Reading Matters described below. Another would be Freedom Road, a project in Hull, working with young people who are either looked after, or on the edge of 'care'. This organisation, initiated and led by children and young people and supported by adults, works with those who are disaffected by school, or who are not in education, employment or training. Using the performing and creative arts, young people are encouraged to raise their aspirations and build up their self-confidence, to start to believe in themselves and in some cases, progress to achieving formal qualifications in drama or music. These are the sorts of schemes that adopt a different, more holistic view of those with whom they work. Those who run them know that all children, whatever their backgrounds, possess strengths and gifts and they recognise the potential of young people – all young people – to contribute something worthwhile to society. An important point here is that they respect the uniqueness of these individual youngsters. They realise that they, and the rest of society, can learn from their particular knowledge and experiences. Moreover, in doing so, and alongside them, they can help shape a society that is more responsive to their needs.

That there *are* alternatives to success other than through achieving good grades at school and being born into more privileged circumstances, is self-evident and amply demonstrated by those who have succeeded against the odds. Examples include world-wide entrepreneurs such as Richard Branson, who, although from a relatively affluent background, was dyslexic and did not excel at school, leaving without going on to university. He nevertheless went on to achieve extraordinary, world-wide financial success and recognition, marketing a variety of different brands, from records to airlines, to trains and broadband. More significantly, Barack Obama, elected President of the United States in 2009 and hence the most powerful man in the world, was brought up in relatively deprived circumstances, had no stable father-figure in his life, and, of course, most notably is black. What Obama and Branson and those like them have in common, however, is an ability to resist the labels that could have attached to them, together with an enduring belief in themselves and their capacity to make a difference, fostered by those around them who recognised their potential and encouraged them in their ambitions. They each possess, in other words, a strong sense of their own individual agency. In Obama's own words:

> We know that many in the inner city are trapped by their own self-destructive behaviours but that those behaviours are not innate. And because of that knowledge, the black community remains convinced that if America finds its will to do so, then circumstances for those trapped in the inner city can be changed, individual attitudes among the poor will change in kind, and the damage can gradually be undone, if not for this generation then at least for the next. (Obama, 2007, p 255)

The potential of education

On an international level, Sen has identified the potential of education, particularly for women, to lift whole communities out of deprivation and act as an aid to development. So too, on a more local, level, education can, as evidence has repeatedly indicated, serve as a powerful means to prevent and address offending behaviour. It is known, for example, that 25% of young offenders, have literacy skills below that of the average seven-year-old and are therefore functionally illiterate, having missed out, for a variety of reasons, on conventional schooling. In addition, 70% of those excluded from school have difficulties in basic literacy skills as do 60% of the prison population as a whole (Clark and Dugdale, 2008). This may be because, as already suggested, our current education system seems irrelevant to many young people and they have voted with their feet in absenting themselves from school. Alternatively, it may be that some have undiagnosed conditions such as dyslexia or visual or auditory problems. Whatever the reason, these figures demonstrate all too clearly how many young people have been failed by the system, which has self-evidently been unable to address their needs. The effect on a young person of being unable to read and write in today's society, with the associated emotions this must engender of feeling excluded from the mainstream, and particularly from our current digital age, can, for most of us, only be imagined. If instead, however, those young people who struggle with literacy and who are at risk of becoming disaffected and marginalised, were targeted for the kind of education that Freire proposed, where their personal knowledge and experience of life formed an integral part of the process, then not only would their reading ability be enhanced, so too would their self-confidence and feelings of self-worth.

The significance for young people of having important relationships with concerned adults in their lives is key. For many or most, this is likely to be with their parents or someone known to the family. For others, however, for a variety of reasons, this is not an option. For these young people, having someone who believes in them and can nurture their self-belief, is crucial. A number of years ago, a cinema advert presented a roll-call of famous people, including Tony Blair. Each of them appeared briefly on the screen, mentioned a name, and smiled broadly. The advert, which was to encourage people to enter the teaching profession, ended with the words 'Everybody remembers a good teacher.'

Reading Matters

For some young people, it is not a teacher they remember, but a volunteer. Reading Matters is an organisation that works with young people who are struggling to read and write. This organisation, founded in 1997, works primarily in secondary schools, although increasingly in other locations, including children's own homes, matching volunteers with school pupils who are either reluctant readers or who are struggling with literacy skills. These pupils are usually from deprived backgrounds and also include a significant proportion from black and minority ethnic groups, including Gypsy and Traveller children. Over a 10-week period, volunteers, who are all trained and accredited, meet twice-weekly with their young person, initially focusing on getting to know them and what they are particularly interested in. Using this information, they engage with the youngsters, playing word games and reading books with them that reflect their interests.

A recent evaluation of Reading Matters, found that pupils gained an average of 15 months in terms of word recognition over the 10-week intervention, together with 10 months for reading comprehension (Tan et al, 2008). What was just as important, however, as the researchers noted, was the increase in self-esteem and confidence displayed by young people as a result of this intervention, something commented on favourably by schools, the young people and parents alike. Significant too, was the 'non-threatening, supportive and non-judgemental environment' that the volunteers created for the young people with whom they engaged, something that was seen to contrast with their school experience. Of particular importance in their findings was the discovery that the young people concerned were not in fact necessarily disaffected by reading itself, but 'were discouraged by the reading they associate with school and the classroom' (Tan et al, 2008). They noted that what Reading Matters offers is a chance to bring closer together young people's 'life worlds' with those provided in school by reading volunteers.

What Reading Matters and other similar schemes throughout the country seem to be providing is of considerable significance. It is offering, in Dyson's terms, (Dyson, 2004) an opportunity for young people to contribute their own unique resources to the learning process, and through the interaction between them and the volunteer, to assign meaning to their learning, something that was clearly lacking for these particular pupils in the classroom. By volunteers taking the time to forge a relationship with these young people, by valuing them as individuals, they feel validated as human beings, included in something worthwhile. They are participants in an encounter to which they themselves have something to bring, and this, not surprisingly, has beneficial repercussions on their levels of self-esteem. As a result, they are more likely to avoid feeling excluded by society and to feel a sense of belonging. They are not mere receptacles of information, deposited in them by teachers, but rather, in Freire's terms, co-producers of their education. In resisting the labels that have been placed on them, they are also able to experience a sense of power, of their own agency. Significantly, too, from a societal point of view, they are less likely to 'drop out', to become involved in crime or other anti-social activity, and more likely to engage positively with society, and make their own individual contribution to it.

The relevance for social welfare

As with education, so we will now consider what these authors have to offer social welfare practice. In writing about 'natives' resisting the oppression of those to whom they were subject, Fanon, for example, spoke of the need for individuals to find common cause with one another, to give collective voice to their experiences, and through mastery of language, to claim power. Leonard, likewise, believed that collective action could enhance identity (Leonard, 1984), but in the case of Fanon, he advocated the use of violence to achieve these ends. Without resorting to such lengths, however, what he is describing, is, effectively, what we have earlier referred to when discussing the potential of service user movements. These groups, whether consisting of 'looked after' children, of those with learning disabilities, or vulnerable older people, are all, in the same way as he describes, resisting labels that have been attributed to them, which have served to deny their felt experiences and their way of being in the world. By taking united action in refusing to go along with these classifications, the agency of individuals is enhanced, they experience themselves as possessing a degree of power, and as having the potential to redefine themselves and their role in society. As Foucault put it, 'Where there is power, there is resistance' (Foucault, 1981, p 95), and through resistance, those who have hitherto been powerless can begin to express their own power. So, instead of seeing themselves merely as passive recipients of welfare services, they can take part in self-help and campaigning activities for improved, more appropriate and more sensitive services (Postle and Beresford, 2007). In addition, by participating in artistic, sporting and other activities, they contribute to a different societal view of themselves, one where they are contributing, often on equal terms, to the general good of society.

In defining the 'praxis', Freire highlighted the importance of reflecting on one's circumstances, a necessary prerequisite, he suggested, to acting on and transforming them. To be able to do this, man needed to believe in himself, a belief that could be brought about through dialogue. Actual self-belief could not, however, be achieved by anyone other than the individual himself. Dialogue could act as an aid, but could not, in itself, bring it about. In other words, Freire was suggesting, as we have done earlier, that empowerment was not something that could be 'done' by those in power to those who lacked it, but rather a process that needed to be worked through by individuals themselves, who, through dialogue, were able to give meaning to the world, to 'name it' and their place within it.

This resonates with the practice, described in an earlier chapter, of narrative therapy, through which individual service users can come to acquire a 'sense of coherence' through translating personal experience into stories. In doing so, they can start to create meaning out of what might otherwise seem to be disorganised, fractured lives. As we noted, and Freire similarly recognised, 'naming the world' and using their own language to do so, can have powerful implications for individuals' sense of identity, for feeling strong rather than weak, and for enhancing a feeling of agency, of being able to act on and shape their circumstances. As such it can prove a particularly effective approach with those service users traditionally cast in passive roles, those who are seen to lack certain abilities or powers that the majority possess, for example, those with learning or other disabilities, vulnerable older people, or some of those receiving family support services. It can also be a means, through dialogue, of challenging defeatist, fatalistic feelings. The person Freire described, who felt he could do nothing as he was 'only a peasant', could be replicated a thousand times over in our encounters with service users, who characteristically often feel helpless and hopeless in the face of the difficult circumstances which they face. Whilst not wishing to suggest that they can transform these conditions overnight, so long as they deny the degree of agency they do possess, they are arguably contributing to their continuation.

Sen and agency

In his writing, Sen argued for a gradualist approach to addressing deprivation and injustice. In defining development as freedom, and freedom as agency, he recognised 'the positive role of free and sustainable agency – and even of constructive impatience' (Sen, 1999a, p 11) in promoting development, and claiming individual rights, such as education and political and economic freedoms. Enhancing agency, moreover, was not only the main object of development, but also the means: the process of development in itself served to enhance individual well-being.

Whilst Sen was clearly writing about societies at a different stage of development from our own, nevertheless, his approach has much to offer us also. He recognised that a two-way relationship between agency and structure not only served to enhance individual happiness, but also produced social arrangements that were more appropriate and effective; and he went further, suggesting that an over-emphasis on income poverty at the expense of other forms of deprivation, such as social exclusion in all its forms, might not be effective, by itself, in enhancing well-being. He argued, therefore, for greater integration of economic, social and political activity, and in doing so, was effectively promoting the kind of 'joined-up' approach that is currently being advocated in our own society to issues relating to the care of children and vulnerable older people.

For Sen, however, although 'responsibility requires freedom', freedom also imposes responsibility. In other words, acquiring agency comes at a price. While not suggesting that 'free' individuals should be entirely self-sufficient, Sen was suggesting that they had a moral duty to co-operate with each other for the common good, to use their agency, and by inference, their knowledge and experiences to try to achieve change, change that would not just benefit themselves, but society as whole. In our social welfare context, this might include, for example, individuals acting together to form self-help groups or user movements; or social workers, with their privileged knowledge of the lives and deprivations of the service users they encounter, using this to press for change, for more responsive and appropriate services.

For both Freire and Sen, education was perceived as the primary means of achieving individual and social change. Freire's own focus was on pedagogy, representing a particular style of teaching and it will be helpful, at this stage, to consider in some detail what he and others before and after him mean by this term and what it may have to offer us.

Social pedagogy

The notion of *social* pedagogy is an approach that is already gaining some currency in Britain. It has its roots in German progressive education and in adopting a holistic approach, starts from a position that is different from conventional education, taking as its focus not just the simple imparting and acquisition of knowledge and information, but rather the whole person, the development of the whole child, and their happiness and well-being. In Belgium, social pedagogy has been described as 'walking in the shoes of' a child, emphasising the empathetic qualities that are a prerequisite of this approach. *Social* pedagogy, as the name implies, views the care of children as the responsibility, not just of parents, but of society as a whole. Partly as a result, it is an approach that frequently underpins community work and education and it is in this way that it is associated with Freire's work. Indeed, his contribution is cited as an example of social pedagogy in action (see Cannan and Warren, 1997).

Petrie et al (2006) have identified nine basic principles of social pedagogy. These include not just a focus on the whole person, but also on the centrality of the relationship between pedagogue and child; the need to see children and those working with them as 'inhabiting the same life space, not as existing in separate domains' and for pedagogues to recognise their own personhood in this encounter; for pedagogues to reflect on their work; and for them to recognise as important what children bring to the encounter from other parts of their life. It is also important to note that these authors emphasise the need to work alongside others who are important in a child's life, not just their parents, but also other figures significant to them in their communities (Petrie et al, 2006).

Central in all the writing about social pedagogy is the emphasis on human dignity, on mutual respect and trust, trust not simply by the child of the pedagogue, but also by the latter of the child themselves. Trust, in this approach, is a two-way affair and, for them to be meaningful, should underpin all therapeutic encounters.

Social pedagogy has been recognised moreover, and not just by Freire, as a powerful tool in fighting social inequalities. Through its holistic approach, it has the potential to change the way we conceptualise those with whom we work, to see them not as 'other', but as people like ourselves. As such, it has much to offer not just to the development of new, more responsive systems of education, but also to social work and approaches to welfare. Cannan has described it as 'a perspective, including social action which aims to promote human welfare through child-rearing and education practices; and to prevent or ease social problems by providing people with the means to manage their own lives, and make changes in their circumstances' (Cannan et al, 1992, pp 73–4). Social pedagogy is, in other words, a means, among other things, of enhancing individual agency. Through its conceptualisation as a way of combating social problems, it has come to be seen as an approach that has much to offer not just to children in an educative context, but to service users more widely, including young offenders and children who are looked after. Its principles could also arguably be applied to all those with whom we work as service users, including vulnerable older people and those with disabilities.

There are, however, potential problems with social pedagogy. As much as it can be seen as a force for the good, it also has the potential to be 'high-jacked' by those in power; and 'as the embodiment of dominant social interests...as a way of taking its values to all sections of the population and exercising more effective social control' (Lorenz, 1994, p 93). However, as the same author points out, it can also be 'the thorn in the flesh of official agenda, an emancipatory programme for self-directed learning processes inside and outside the education system geared towards the transformation of society' (Lorenz, 1994, p 93). If the second of these approaches is seen as its role, it can indeed be a powerful tool in the hands of educators and social workers alike.

The recent interest in social pedagogy in our own society and in what it might have to offer may well be associated with its focus on well-being. This is, in itself, a topic currently attracting considerable attention, reflected in the number of books recently published, addressing happiness and well-being from a number of different angles (e.g. Layard, 2005; Wilkinson and Pickett, 2009). Alongside this literature, and perhaps in part prompting it, has been the sobering awareness, arising from the UNICEF report (2007), that despite our relative affluence, children living in Britain are among the unhappiest in the world. Current research, commissioned by the Department of Children, Schools and Families, and taking as its focus children 'on the edge of care' and mainstream parenting support, has, for example, recommended building on the ideas presented in the social pedagogical approach, particularly in residential work with looked after children. Specifically, it advocates the '(social pedagogic) objective: to support the young person's upbringing and education-in-the-broadest-sense' (Boddy et al, 2009). It also 'highlighted the potential of social pedagogy as a qualification for therapeutic intervention with young people and families', and suggests that future development work builds on the residential social care pilot of social pedagogy and includes social pedagogues (as well as psychologists) in child welfare teams (Boddy et al, 2009). The Children's Workforce Development Council (CWDC) also acknowledged, in a report produced in early 2009 (CWDC, 2009), the potential of training in social pedagogy, recommending 'consideration of the key principles of social pedagogy and integrating these within the standards [of residential care]'. In these various ways, the potential contribution of social pedagogy is increasingly being recognised and beginning to influence practice.

Social work and political engagement

Fanon, Freire and Sen all demonstrated a clear political commitment to the societies about which they wrote. So, too, social work should be recognised as being, in part, also a political activity, something that has been observed by a number of authors in the past. Howe, for example, stated that '[equally] important is the recognition that, like education, social work *is* politics, and necessarily means political activity' (Howe, 1987, p 128). He goes on to quote Davies (Davies, 1982) who, citing Freire's idea that education should aim at fundamental change, suggested that what is true for education, is true also for social work. Referring to Davies' work, he says 'the goal of education and welfare is to "politicise" learners and clients [sic] to the point where they can see the need and value of gaining power for themselves' (Howe, 1987, p 129).

The undermining of social work

This view has gone markedly out of fashion in recent times. Instead, social workers are arguably more concerned today both with meeting government agendas that focus on achieving measurable results and which may or may not seem relevant either to social workers or to service users; and on trying to 'cover their backs', to ensure that forms are filled in, risk assessments completed, and routine procedures followed, so that they and their departments will avoid association with the type of tragedies and consequent adverse media coverage that have come to be all too readily associated with social work recently. As has been noted elsewhere, 'social work...has largely lost sight of its political role in promoting social inclusion, citizenship and social justice' (Postle and Beresford, 2007, p 152).

The frenetic, defensive activity now demanded of social workers moreover allows little time for reflection or analysis of the 'bigger picture', of thinking about what social work is essentially there to achieve. Indeed, what used to be termed 'supervision', but is now more commonly referred to as 'case management' tends to be exactly that: a managerial overview of the 'cases' held by a front-line worker, including whether or not basic legal requirements are being fulfilled in terms of frequency of visits and the like; whether any costs can be saved by, for example, moving a child or adult to a cheaper placement; or whether the 'case' can be closed. The opportunity afforded by erstwhile supervision sessions to think in depth about the social worker's involvement with service users, to analyse their interaction, to interpret behaviour and to consider unmet and perhaps unvoiced needs, and what might lie behind the 'presenting problem', has all but disappeared.

This departure marks a break, not just with client–centred approaches or those described by Howe as 'the seekers after meaning', but also with radical social work, two of the main schools of thought that we described earlier. So should we conclude, therefore, that social work has thrown the baby out with the bathwater, leaving itself morally and professionally bankrupt, a mere poodle in the hands of political administrations of whatever hue?

This conclusion would, in fact, be most unfair. Anecdotal evidence suggests instead that social workers feel deeply frustrated by what they perceive as the hijacking of their professional agenda. They resent the downplaying of their expertise, the assumption that social work is merely 'common sense'. They sense that their engagement and relationship skills are seen as redundant and to a great extent being ignored in favour of mechanistic approaches to achieving targets. They also lament the fact that a disproportionate amount of their time is taken up with the bureaucracy involved in chasing and demonstrating these targets, time that is then no longer available for meeting with service users. These targets have moreover, usually been drawn up without reference to social workers and certainly not to service users themselves. They are, instead, devised by those in power, who tend to view service recipients as 'other', as 'objects to be studied' and 'problems to be solved' Social workers, however, know that what is being measured often bears little relationship to the realities and concerns faced by service users and that the criteria against which they are judged are often spurious. As has been noted elsewhere, 'the real focus is on performance indicators chosen for ease of measurement and control rather than because they measure accurately what the *quality* of performance is' (O'Neill, 2002, p 54, emphasis added).

For social workers, however, those with whom they work are people about whom they care deeply, not mere statistics. They know that, ultimately, happiness and well-being cannot easily be measured, that the relationships they build with service users are often not only a means to an end, but for many people, an end in themselves and as such, should not be disregarded. It is their skills in relating to people from a whole variety of backgrounds, of sharing their concerns and assisting them, by whatever means, in making changes, that social workers' interests and expertise lie. And unlike others, social workers also have a sense of their service users as subjects of their own lives, as people, who, whether or not they conceptualise it in this way, possess agency.

Social work's mediating role

This knowledge takes us back nearly to where we started from. As we noted in an earlier chapter, Philp, in his influential article, identified the crucial role of social workers as people who perhaps alone, could represent service users' lives to those in power and who could bring to life their humanity (Philp, 1979). Operating in the space in between the individual and society, in 'the delicate interface' between the two, part of the role of social workers is essentially to bring to subjectivity the lives of those with whom they work, the people who are so easily objectified by those in power. It is social workers who have this duty, this responsibility, and ultimately this political role.

For social workers to achieve this, however, they too need to see themselves as subjects, as people who can influence the systems within which they operate. They need, in essence, to recognise, to believe in and to use their own sense of agency. So how can they achieve this, and what means can they employ to do this most effectively?

It is interesting to note at this point, in our postmodern society, with its movement away from grand narratives, from overarching ideas and the belief that scientific ideas can 'solve' our problems, that recent administrations do not seem to have caught up with this. Instead, they seem locked in a time-warp, where 'big ideas' are still very much in evidence, where power is centralised in the hands of a few, and where, for example, in education and social work, the agenda is imposed from above. As Power has commented 'the growth of auditing has been the explosion of an idea, an idea that has become central to a certain style of controlling individuals and which has permeated organisational life' (1997). In the 'audit society' that Power describes, the collation and analysis of statistical data and performance indicators are seen as the primary means of 'solving' social problems and people's personal accounts of the circumstances they themselves are best-placed to understand, are rarely heard. Instead, reliance is placed on inspections and audits and on the results that they supposedly reveal. This approach is largely at odds with many of the rest of society's institutions, where, in our cultural pursuits, in sport, in our burgeoning ethnic groupings and in our family patterns, plurality and diversity are now generally welcomed and embraced. In this wider world, individual voices are increasingly heard, difference is celebrated, and personal information is welcomed, if not seized upon, in some newspapers and reality TV shows.

One of the most significant ways this has been achieved is through the media and increasingly through the internet. The internet and other associated technology, as has of course been widely recognised, have indeed changed our lives enormously. One of the ways they have done so has been through the creation of 'virtual' communities, bringing together those with similar interests, or backgrounds to share experiences and ideas. In this way, by putting people in touch with each other, information is disseminated and cascaded, and through these means reaches out to and influences potentially a huge number of people.

Political methods

Using new technology and the media more effectively provides one possible way in which social workers and others can begin to disseminate their own particular knowledge and experience, to bring to a wider audience the realities of service users' lives, to exercise their own particular political power. They could, for example, participate, individually or collectively, in the kind of idea exemplified by 'Comment is free', the brainchild of *The Guardian*, a website read apparently by millions each month, and forging 'something powerful, plural and diverse' from 'combining a newspaper's columnists with those other voices' (Rusbridger, 2009). They might, for example, by using this website or through similar mechanisms, such as writing collectively to newspapers, choose to react to news items that relate to or have a bearing on their work, where a considered professional viewpoint might have a powerful corrective potential, when the reality, has, in their eyes, been misrepresented. When, for example, a young person commits a particularly unpleasant offence, it could be salutary for social workers, using the media, to emphasise and bring to the wider world's attention the kind of situation in which he is likely to have grown up, his possible lack of education, the social exclusion he has probably faced, and to put forward some positive ideas and examples of how these deprivations might be tackled in future and help limit the likelihood of others committing similar crimes. In the aftermath of an offence such as the murder of James Bulger, for example, numerous voices typically clamour to be heard, most of them ill-informed but anxious to contribute their views to the debate, their analysis of what is wrong with society. In such a situation the views of social workers and probation officers are rarely acknowledged or given credence, despite being arguably better informed than most reporters or spokespeople, who are nevertheless readily afforded air-time or newspaper inches. Through more concerted effort however, the voices of front-line social workers could be put to good effect, by placing such an offence in its social context, by attempting to mitigate the inevitable blame, and by helping those who do not come from the standpoint of holding professional knowledge, to try to understand some of the reasons behind such behaviour.

Similarly, social workers might also choose, individually or collectively, to approach councillors or their MP, if they become aware of particular issues that concern them and which have an impact on service users at a local level. They might, for example, in an area of high-density housing, where the incidence of road traffic accidents affecting children is particularly high and where there are no gardens and little public play space, lobby for 20mph speed limits in residential roads, where children play out. Similarly, they might want to press for more road crossings and, alongside teachers, for walking buses to and from school. In a similar vein, they could make out a case to their own department for money to be allocated to family support services that include as part of their brief, addressing road safety awareness for both parents and children, and also make approaches to schools to include safety ranger programmes as part of their Personal, Social and Health Education (PSHE) curriculum, provided perhaps in partnership with the police. The possibilities are clearly endless, but all of them depend on social workers exercising their own sense of agency, their own 'constructive impatience' (Sen, 1999a) to bring about change, using what power they possess responsibly to build on the structures that shape service users' and their own lives.

The voice of service users

Social workers should not, however, simply rely on their own sense of agency to effect change. Instead, and potentially more effectively, the voices of service users themselves need to be heard in the political arena. It is they who, after all, experience most clearly and directly the effects of social policy, of the education system, of housing and social security provision, and who can – and indeed should – potentially exert most power and influence in transforming services to better meet their needs.

One way this can be achieved is through the current government focus on participation, on giving service users a voice and 'building their capacity'. Throughout social and community services, there is now an emphasis on hearing the views of those on the receiving end, on encouraging users to help shape and deliver services and to give feedback as to their effectiveness or otherwise. These are opportunities that should not be missed of giving service users a voice, even if, as might sometimes be the case, what they have to say is not always what the government expects or wants to hear. Indeed, this feedback may have the potential of delivering unintended consequences for an administration that seems to be seeking ever more centralised control!

There are other ways, though, of service users having a voice. Holman has written consistently over a number of years of his work with fellow residents on the Easterhouse estate in Glasgow. In *Faith in the poor* (Holman, 1998) he writes movingly of the need to read the words, not of the wrong, but of 'the right writers', those who actually live in Easterhouse. Indeed, much of his book is given over to individuals' personal accounts of their experiences, the meaning their lives hold for them, the difficulties with which they have to cope, and above all the resilience they have shown in dealing with what life has placed at their door. The focus of this particular book is individuals' experiences of poverty. Of equal significance, however, might be one that addressed different individuals' experiences of, for example, domestic violence. What Holman brings out very vividly in this book, and indeed, the motivating force behind it, is the refusal of usual communication outlets to give people in these sorts of circumstances a voice. Although those who contribute to the book acknowledge the existence of their negative feelings, 'they do, at times, react with a determination to fight back' (Holman, 1998, p 166).

The lives of the individuals recording their experiences in this book could, as Holman recognises, have been presented, by other authors, in very different, objective terms: as heroin addicts or prostitutes; or as work-shy young people, whose lack of morality could pose a threat to others (Holman, 1998, pp 8–9). What they are offered in Holman's book, however, is an opportunity to demonstrate the meaning which their lives hold for them, and to demonstrate their shared humanity. He is, in other words, presenting them as the subjects of their own lives. After receiving some of the 'right' kind of help, 'Carol' talked about what she felt the government should do to address the problems of Easterhouse residents. 'But', she added, 'we must act as well...because the community needs to be for each other' (Holman, 1998, p 49).

It is this kind of opportunity that we should, alongside service users themselves, be seeking out: the chance to catch a glimpse of the person behind the statistic, the teenager who, like others his age, has his hopes and dreams, but who, for a whole variety of reasons, some personal to him alone, some shared with others, believes he cannot achieve them. By helping him to tell his story, giving him the opportunity to say what his life means to him, he not only begins to feel empowered, but, if his voice is heard in the right places, may start to open doors for himself and others.

This might come about, as with the residents of Easterhouse, through him writing about his life; it may be that he chooses to communicate through art, as with the young people of Kids Company in London; or it might be through creative use of the internet that he tells his story. He might be someone who has no interest or aptitude in any of these areas, but who, given the chance, could excel on the football pitch or in the swimming pool and talk about the effect this might have on his life and aspirations. Ultimately, it is up to him to tell his story in his own way – and for those in touch and perhaps working with him, to 'walk in his shoes' and help him to do so.

Conclusion

In this chapter, we initially moved away from local concerns to consider what other authors, writing from different periods and perspectives and about other cultures, may have to offer. We were introduced, in Fanon's writing about colonialism, to the notion and possibility of resistance; and by Freire, to his belief in the power of education, and, in this context, to the importance of dialogue and reflection. Finally, in the work of Sen, we learned that in his view, development is freedom, and that freedom for him, means individual agency.

What all these influential authors share and express in their writing is a strong reaction against determinist views of human behaviour, against those beliefs that suggest the future as well as the present are 'givens', that they are not, in other words, susceptible to alteration by human activity or agency. Sen, for example, puts this strongly when he asserts that, on the contrary, things do change and 'choices do exist; the possibility of reasoning does too...nothing imprisons the mind as much as a false belief in an unalterable lack of choice and the impossibility of reasoning' (Sen, 1999b, p 27). These authors are, above all else, optimists, who believe in the potential for change, change that can be brought about by individuals acting by themselves or collectively within society.

We moved on from this to examine the relevance of these authors' ideas to our own culture and particularly to education and social work; and to explore how the notion of social pedagogy may be relevant in this context. Finally, we considered the political role of social work, and the responsibility we share to present those we work with as subjects of their own lives and how this might be achieved, both by service users and ourselves.

In the Conclusion, we will be attempting to draw together the ideas explored so far and to consider their significance for social work training and the profession as a whole.

FIVE

Conclusion

At one extreme [the person] may be seen simply as an agent responding to the push and pull of forces exerted by the environment. At the other, he may be seen as an agent guiding his behaviour toward some explicit goal by some means of which he is thoroughly aware. (Harre and Secord, 1972, p 8)

[T]he emphasis on structure...only tells half the story. In order to explain how men and women make history in particular circumstances we need an account sensitive enough to disentangle human agency from structural effect. (Mann, 1985, p 72)

Introduction

Throughout this book, the focus has been on individual agency, on its philosophical origins, its development as a concept particularly in the fields of sociology and social policy and specifically, on its potential for illuminating our work with service users. In presenting agency in this way, we have referred also to the relationship between agency and structure, to the dynamic interaction between the two, and to the potential of individuals, using their own knowledge and experiences, to have an impact on societal structures.

Agency is however, an elusive concept that is hard to pin down. In recent years it has, in fact, come to acquire inappropriate, individualistic connotations, being seen by some as primarily related to the achievement of personal goals, of individual rights and freedoms and associated with the idea of choice rather than with change (Hoggett, 2001, p 52). This, however, is, at best, to misunderstand and at worst deliberately to misrepresent what agency can mean. Indeed, it arguably represents a hijacking of the concept, by those either on the right or left of the political divide – an attempt to appropriate it for specific factional gain. Indeed, in this context, the idea of agency can be reduced to a point of absurdity – where individuals are perceived as significant purely in their role as consumers, and only insofar as they are capable of exercising choice between different brands.

Choosing how to behave, which particular road to follow and what methods to adopt in, for example, professional practice with service users, are of course, all aspects of individual agency in operation. However, its overriding significance as a concept lies, in contrast, in its relationship qualities. It is through communicative interaction with others, through our general sociability as human beings and our relationship with society and its constituent structures that agency needs to be viewed and its potential recognised. As Parton and O'Byrne recognised, agency assumes relationship (2000) and it is this overarching quality of agency that we have been attempting to highlight and illuminate.

In the remaining part of this book, and bearing this in mind, we will be focusing first on the key qualities of individual agency that we have been attempting to emphasise and in conclusion, on the implications for social work training.

Agency: a way forward?

In the early part of this book, we acknowledged the importance of certain influential social work authors. These included Biestek (1961), Halmos (1965) and in particular, Raymond Plant (1970). We noted how, in his writing, Plant highlighted the paramount importance in social work practice of respecting service users (Plant, 1970). It had already been recognised that this was essential if any work with them was to be effective (for example, Biestek, 1961), but Plant went further. Focusing on the ethical justification for social work, he argued that an individual's moral agency was their transcendent feature, that the inherent rationality of all human beings demanded that they should not be subject to manipulation, but had a right to self-direction and self-determination. Along with this right to respect and self-determination, Plant argued, came responsibility: the need for individuals not merely to react passively to external circumstances, but to respond actively to them. Writing from a very different perspective, this was also recognised by Sen, who, while arguing that 'responsibility requires freedom', also emphasised that freedom itself imposes responsibility (Sen, 1999a).

Respect

It is the interpretation of respect, something owed to individuals purely because of their shared humanity that we have also been trying to emphasise. In this sense, the users of social services should arguably be viewed as no different to those who benefit from other professions. In medicine, in religion and in the eyes of the law, all members of society, all citizens, whatever their background and circumstances are, after all, considered equal in their right to treatment, to legal representation and to worship, and in this sense, are recognised as sharing a common humanity. Whilst this does not in itself serve to eliminate health inequalities, for example, nevertheless it provides a basis from which these rights can be claimed. In a democracy like ours, those with whom social work engages should also share these rights. Social work, in other words, should now be claiming equal status to that of other professions, not just in its own interests but also in the interests of those with whom it engages.

The role of the social worker here is crucial. Through our work, we come to know service users as 'subjects' not 'objects', to have some understanding of their lives. We are therefore in a position to present them as people, as individuals who have a voice, a right to have their say and be heard. It is our role therefore, as Philp recognised, to act as mediators between them and society, to demonstrate their subjectivity to those who need to listen, to bring alive their experiences and the hardship they so often face. In this sense, social work is not only an interpersonal activity but as we have argued, essentially a political one also.

Individual meaning

In addition, we have a responsibility to assist and enable service users themselves to convey to others the reality of their own circumstances, the meaning they place on their own lives. Agency is after all concerned also with meaning, particularly the significance that individuals' lives hold for them. So, instead of being viewed in objective terms, and seen, for example, simply as young offenders or as belonging to a particular ethnic group, service users, helped by those working with them can, where they choose to do so, resist these attributions, present their own personal accounts and by so doing, gain in self-respect. In the context of social work practice, this might be through individuals creating narratives that hold particular meaning for them, or, for example, in supporting families via a strengths-based approach. It might relate to the prisoner who has been introduced to studying through the Open University, who although in custody, sees himself less as a prisoner and more as a student. It is an argument, in other words, for approaches that put a value on individual meaning, on personal interaction and on research methods that rely on qualitative as well as quantitative methods, ones that describe the realities of people's everyday lives, as well as those that involve gathering objective statistical data about them.

As we have suggested, this meaning might best be conveyed to a wider audience in artistic ways, perhaps by literally creating dramas out of crises, or through representational art or in writing about personal experience, as the residents of Easterhouse did in Holman's *Faith in the poor* (Holman, 2001). For, as some have observed, the arts have an important role to play in the depiction of different people's lives, in honouring their experience and celebrating the 'otherness' in them that we can ultimately recognise in ourselves (for example, Eyre, 2005).

Self-belief

By recognising and validating the meaning individuals' lives hold for them, they are more likely to believe in themselves and in their own potential. The belief that they, like others, can have an impact on their circumstances and effect change is, as we have noted, an essential aspect of agency. Through interaction with others, by 'naming' their own world and their own experiences, individuals may come to realise more clearly what is important to them, and that they have the power, particularly alongside others, to influence and shape their future. For some service users, their relationship with social or community workers may be the first genuine opportunity they have had to reflect on their lives, on their behaviour and its meaning and to consider what changes they can make to help achieve the future they want for themselves. The same teenager who helps put together a film depicting her inner-city life might, for example, discover that she has an aptitude for camera work and, as a result, feel able to sign up for a course to pursue film-making. Alternatively, another of these young people may use the confidence gained from this success to branch out in a different direction, rather than settle for a life of unemployment or a dead-end job. In a different context, this is also what Freire referred to as the 'praxis', the ability of individuals to reflect on their situation, and to realise that it is not immutable, but something that they themselves can act upon and transform (Freire, 1970).

Identity

Enhanced self-belief is moreover, closely allied with a more robust sense of identity. In viewing himself as a student, as someone who is using his time creatively and constructively, the prisoner is more likely to hold on to and build on his self-esteem, and correspondingly less likely to see himself as being merely a prisoner. In doing so, not only will his sense of identity and agency be enhanced, he is also more likely to avoid the 'learned helplessness' and institutionalisation characterised by many in custody, who come to accept their circumstances passively, with an associated loss of self-esteem and tendency towards depression (Seligman, 1975). Similarly, children and young people who are physically or sexually harmed, if offered appropriate and timely therapy in the aftermath of the abuse, by someone whom they can trust, are more likely to avoid long-term damage and to move on. They may even, with this help, reach a point where they can help others who have suffered in the same way. They may, in other words, in avoiding the feeling of helplessness that can so often accompany abuse, be able to experience a sense of their own agency and use this to help transform someone else's life in the future.

Resilience

What the student prisoner and the children who have been abused are demonstrating in their contrasting situations is a sense of resilience, a 'refusal to accept their fate' (Frost and Hoggett, 2008, p 7). They are resisting the labels that others might ascribe to them, refusing to accept themselves as others might see them and instead are acting as subjects of their own lives. In doing so, they are moving on from the circumstances by which others might choose to define them and 'abandoning the imprint of the past' (Cyrulnik, cited by Groskop, 2009). Essentially, in other words, they are discovering new meaning in their lives and fighting back.

   In resisting the labels that others attach to them they are also allowing themselves to hope, to believe in the possibility of a positive future. Instead of acquiescing in the idea of a future that for them is pre-determined and offers little, of being, in Freire's terms, complicit in their own oppression, they are starting to believe that they are capable of change.

Negative agency

We must remain aware, however, that there will always be some service users who do not behave in this way. There are those who exercise their agency in negative ways, whose behaviour, like that of the repeat offender, appears to us not to be in their best interests, but who just find that, for them, crime pays off. They may be people whose behaviour is in no real sense reasoned, but the result of acting on impulse, a response to difficult circumstances, in which rational choice has no real part to play.

There are others too who choose not to resist their circumstances but simply to accept their lot. In choosing acceptance, they are, however, also exercising agency. The patient dying of cancer may appear, and in many ways be, very powerless and dependent, but in their particular situation this can also be constructive. Sometimes just being is simply more important than doing, and fighting against death till the bitter end is not always the most heroic course of action (Hoggett, 2001).

Effectively then, we need to view service users, as being, like ourselves, a mixture of conflicting emotions, with different aspects of the self and different priorities taking precedence at different times. In respecting people as individuals, we are accepting that they are capable of behaviour that is often inconsistent, which sometimes appears to others (but not necessarily themselves) to be at odds with their best interests, but that they are also capable of change, if this is something they themselves choose (Hoggett, 2001).

As social workers, we need to hold on to this idea, to the belief that in those with whom we engage there is always something to which we can connect. Indeed, if this were not the case, there would, as Hoggett notes 'be no basis for any kind of therapeutic alliance'. We need, as Hoggett continues, to believe that, even in the most desperate of situations, we are engaging with those who are themselves 'capable of glimpsing hope and life beyond the despair and torment' (Hoggett, 2001, p 53).

Agency and relationship

How social workers then relate to service users is crucial. For, as we recognised at the beginning of this conclusion, relationships are at the heart of what makes social work distinctive. Indeed, they are essentially its raison d'être. For a vulnerable older person, living alone and dependent on others to care for her, it is not just whether the district nurse arrives and changes her dressings regularly, or whether her meals on wheels are tasty and arrive on time, it is the relationships she has with those involved in the delivery of these services that are important, and fundamental to her level of well-being. However efficiently her wounds are dressed, however well cooked and promptly delivered her meals are, if the people involved in these services do not relate to her as an individual and treat her respectfully, she will not, quite simply, be happy. If they view her merely as just another elderly client whose needs must be addressed as quickly as possible in the interests of efficiency, then she will be upset, might start to feel a nuisance, and will begin to lose her self-respect. She might start to feel in the way, less entitled to assistance than others whom she views as perhaps more important. She will, in essence, start to experience herself as an object.

The current business culture within social work, with its emphasis on achieving targets and outcomes means, however, that the significance of these kinds of respectful relationships is in danger of being lost. It has recently been observed that in one local government agency, 'social workers spent 60% of every day in front of a computer safeguarding their information trails, rather than doing the job of looking after children' (Jenkins, 2010). In situations such as this, the need to be seen to achieve measurable outcomes is arguably considered more important than the work itself. Ironically, too, it is often not the outcome so much as the process that is of primary importance to the service user herself. As a recent critic of government policy expressed it, 'What matters to us aren't the figures we're fed, or the targets that get hit, but what the experience feels like to us...the business of all public services is dealing with the needs of people, and...those are never just mechanical, but social and emotional too' (Russell, 2009).

This is not, however, to suggest that services should not aim to be efficient, or that we should squander resources unnecessarily by failing to analyse where and how best they should be spent. This would be tantamount to throwing out the baby with the bath water. Instead, what is being suggested is an approach that attempts to redress the balance, which does justice to both process *and* outcome, to qualitative as well as quantitative research, to subjective experience as well as to what objective data reveals. This is an approach that, while acknowledging the contribution the latter can offer, recognises that social care is an art at least as much as a science. It is an encounter between individuals, rather than merely a means of achieving an outcome. It celebrates diversity and otherness, rather than imposing conformity. It is an approach too, that, instead of trying to cling on to the certainties of the past, is rooted in our own uncertain, postmodern times, which celebrates human beings in all their difference, in all their variety, and embraces the possibility of change.

These aspects of individual agency that we have argued are so important in our dealings with service users are, indeed, equally important for social workers. For us to be able to work in a way that promotes and enhances individual agency in service users, we, too, need to demonstrate these qualities, to have a sense of self-belief, to demonstrate resilience, and, importantly, to model the kind of relationships which we are trying to promote in those with whom we work.

In the final section we will therefore be considering the implications for social work training of adopting an approach that recognises agency as central.

Agency: the relevance for training and practice in social care

The threat to social work values

We have already noted the current centrally-driven preoccupation with measurement and outcomes and the associated focus on achieving targets. In the context of social work training, this has had considerable impact on the syllabus in terms of teaching content with, as Batsleer and Humphreys recognised, social work training moving 'away from critical analysis of the social and political construction of knowledge towards prescription and imposition of a narrowly-defined curriculum based on approved pre-selection of knowledge and skills' (Batsleer and Humphreys, 2000, p 6). It has also informed the way students themselves are assessed. Today, there is far more emphasis on quantifiable means of student assessment, on measuring their performance using tick box methods and techniques, arguably at the expense of 'whole person' approaches and evaluation methods. There is correspondingly less scope in today's syllabus for discussion, for exploring ideas, and sharing experience.

This emphasis on measurement and targets perhaps reflects a deeper change in our society, one that values form over content, substance more than essence, and ultimately structure above agency. This is arguably apparent in our societal preoccupation with celebrity, appearance and conspicuous consumption. In a social work context this results in a loss of focus on what is arguably the fundamental value and content of social work. It is this that training should perhaps now be addressing, to ensure it does not become simply another means of assessing, controlling and 'treating' individuals, with a view to them fitting more neatly into existing societal structures. Instead, we need a greater emphasis on our core values to ensure that students are not being trained just to be efficient technocrats, but professionals who can empathise with service users, who can 'walk in their shoes'. After all, as Jordan put it, social workers do not in the end 'deliver' care, they either do care or they don't care (Jordan, 2003). So with these considerations in mind, in what ways does professional training need to change?

Agency theory, as we have tried to demonstrate, arguably represents the point at which sociology, philosophy, psychology and psychoanalytic theory converge and interconnect. It has also informed thinking about economics and international development, as we have seen, for example, in the work of Sen. It is perhaps this widespread relevance and connectivity that lends agency theory much of its force. To provide a basis for addressing agency then, it is suggested first that ethics and values are afforded a far more central place within the curriculum. A variety of authors (for example, Plant, 1970; Horne, 1987; Banks, 2006) have made considerable contributions to an understanding of this area and their work would provide a useful starting point. Recent recognition of the need to return to an ethical focus for social work was indeed amply demonstrated by the huge numbers who subscribed to two national conferences, on 'Affirming our value base' (Nottingham 2006, 2008). Those who attended included not just older practitioners but also many from a newer, younger generation of professionals. Evidence such as this suggests that the introduction of additional content and discussion about the ethical basis of social work is indeed overdue.

The contribution of sociological theory

Second, sociological theory needs to be more fully represented on professional courses. Analysing the contributions made by, for example, the early Marx, Sartre and Giddens would, as Ferguson notes, help to locate individual issues more clearly within their social context (Ferguson, 2008). He points out that while other disciplines, such as psychology and political science, have recently been focusing more on economic inequality, social work has been moving away from structural issues to a greater focus on the individual, specifically on individual pathology. As Beck argues, however, it is important that the 'problems of the system' are not allowed to be 'transformed into personal failure' (Beck, 1993). On the contrary, as Ferguson goes on to suggest 'reclaiming a structural understanding of society in the form of a critical sociology...is an essential task in reconstructing a social work practice capable of grasping the totality of service users' lives' (attributed to Simpson and Price, 2007, cited in Ferguson, 2008, p 135).

The history of social work has indeed been characterised by an overemphasis at different stages, on either society or the individual, with the interdependence between individual experience and societal structure being, as a result, largely overlooked. As Williams et al have observed, 'the relationships between notions of identity, subjectivity, agency and socio-economic circumstances remain largely untheorised' (Williams et al, 1999, p 159). We need then to move away from this type of binary thinking, of focusing on *either* the individual *or* society, on structure *or* agency, to find a way of challenging such dichotomies, allowing for multiple and interdependent ways of enhancing our understanding. We need, in other words, an approach that can consider more effectively both the external structural constraints on a person's life, such as poverty, homelessness, and unemployment, together with the impact these have on them as individuals and how this in turn influences their view of themselves and their place in the world.

Service users' experiences

Third, therefore, there should be a greater focus on the experiences of service users themselves, on their individual lives and on what we can learn from their particular accounts. As Sen suggested, we need to recognise not just the effects of poverty on individuals, but also the emotional impact on them of feeling socially excluded (Sen, 1999a). We need, in other words, not just to learn how best to work *with* people but also how to learn *from* them. Service users could, for example, contribute directly to a number of curriculum areas, including, for example, child protection, mental health and disability, outlining for example, the issues that brought them into contact with professionals, and their feelings about being in receipt of services. In drawing on their knowledge we would not only be learning from them, but also effectively validating both their personal experience and the service users themselves. In this way, they might start to feel a sense of their own agency and an awareness of the impact they can have on the structures around them. In this instance they could, for example, influence in the longer term the way the social work curriculum is understood and taught.

The emphasis on what service users themselves bring to their encounter with professionals could be enhanced by including references in training to social pedagogy and where it might be relevant. Whilst pedagogical approaches have, so far, been adopted for the most part by those involved in education and residential work, they have additional potential, as we have recognised, for engaging service users from a number of different backgrounds, including young offenders, vulnerable older people and those with mental health problems. Whilst it is important to recognise that social pedagogy is a separate discipline from social work, nevertheless exploring some of these ideas while in training could encourage future social workers to be open to what pedagogical approaches have to offer.

The role of the arts

Alongside the direct accounts of service users' lives there could, as we have recognised, be a greater reliance on what social work students can learn from the imaginative arts. By reading and discussing relevant films or works of fiction, and 'getting inside' the characters of those suffering from mental illness, or those who are losing capacity through the slow onset of Alzheimer's disease, for example, students could enhance their understanding of these conditions and be better placed to respond to them sensitively and appropriately when they later encounter them in their work. By being open to what people, real or fictional, have to tell us about their experiences, we can increase our own understanding of how best to engage with them.

Binary thinking is not only apparent in the focus, already described, on either the individual or society. It is also present in the sometimes fraught relationships that exist between residential and field workers and between the statutory and voluntary sectors. In this context, there is often rivalry, antagonism and a misunderstanding of the equally important roles played by staff in other settings or sectors. One possible departure from the conventional curriculum might therefore take the form of students going out to visit contrasting types of work setting, to residential homes, day centres, and to agencies run not just by the local authority but also the voluntary, community and faith sector and by private companies. In doing so, students would gain some understanding of what both the statutory and the voluntary sector, and residential and field workers can provide, and a realisation that in each case, both are potentially equally important and can be complementary.

An emphasis on change

Alongside these suggested additions to the curriculum could be included a focus on change and how it occurs. Change of one sort or another is, after all, one of the major outcomes that social workers are trying to achieve. An approach like this could effectively bring together insights from different disciplines such as sociology and psychology and serve to demonstrate how structure and agency interact to transform society, and the lives of those individuals within it. A focus on these ideas, along with the others outlined above, might also enable social work students to understand what part they and service users can play, through using their own agency, in helping to achieve change. This is particularly important in the current climate, where social workers may feel at the mercy of the media whenever things go wrong, and held personally accountable if, for example, a child known to them dies at the hands of his parents or others. An awareness of the potential of individual agency in this context might be helpful, encouraging social workers to believe that things can be different, that circumstances do change and that they can be instrumental in achieving this.

The belief that things can indeed move on and be different is in fact fundamental if positive change is to occur. Without this, too many social workers are likely to fall into one of the positions described at the beginning of Chapter Two: to become either the victims of 'compassion fatigue' on the one hand, tending towards a technocratic view of the work where service users are merely routinely visited and assessed and any true sense of engagement with them is lost; or to develop a cynical perspective on society and social work in which everything is seen as hopeless, with neither they nor service users being able to do anything to improve the situation.

Once students move into the workplace, it is vital in both their own interests and the interests of those with whom they work, that they retain a sense of optimism and a belief that change is possible. However, for this to happen, various fundamentals again need to be in place.

The need for supervision

First of all, practitioners need access to regular skilled supervision, to give them the opportunity to share with a senior member of staff from the same professional background the issues that concern them, to reflect on their work in a safe office environment, on what might or might not have gone well, to consider possible different ways of proceeding and to receive informed guidance and support. For, just as social workers will be encouraging service users to reflect on their lives, on what they want to achieve, so they too need the opportunity to do this for themselves. Providing this space, the opportunity to think things through and to share their work with a skilled supervisor is therefore essential, not just in the interests of the worker, but also to try to ensure safe practice and to support the worker in their professional development, to reinforce their own sense of agency.

This style of supervision should be recognised as different from management, where the emphasis is more likely to be driven by departmental priorities and resource considerations. Supervision should have the needs of the worker and their service users firmly at the forefront, with other issues left for another forum.

Additionally, social workers should, in the same way as students, have continuing opportunities to consider other methods of service delivery, of visiting alternative service providers who perhaps do things differently. If they are to be able to work in true partnership with others, they need to be aware that there is more than one way to achieve the same ends, that the same size does not fit all, that each of the different sectors potentially has something equally valid to offer.

Within the hierarchies that inevitably develop within departments, there is arguably a case for employing experienced staff effectively to act as two-way communicators: to serve as a conduit between those who work directly with service users and those who have ultimate responsibility at a managerial or directorate level, for delivering services. By facing both ways, and keeping in close touch with the issues that emerge at the front line, these staff would be best placed to represent the interests of service users to those who are charged at the highest level with addressing their needs. In this way, the dynamic interaction between agency and structure would be facilitated, the lives of those in receipt of services would assume more reality to those in power, and services would hopefully be developed that were more responsive to their needs.

Conclusion

For those looking for guidance on how to 'do' social work, or for advice on social work technique, this book will no doubt have proved a disappointment. Producing such a work was, however, never the intention; it was never meant to be a practical manual, a 'how to do it' guide to social care. Rather, it has been an attempt to look beyond the actual practice of social work, to reconsider what it is we are trying to achieve, to revisit the ethical and moral foundations of our practice and to consider how far agency theory might be able to inform this thinking.

Indeed, agency has increasingly been recognised as having something to offer to social work practice. As Ferguson commented, issues relating to human agency 'have begun to move to the centre of social policy and social work analysis' (Ferguson, 2003, p 199). Others, too, have welcomed the new debate about agency, viewing it as offering opportunities to be 'more sensitive to the activities of poor people, while reflecting more fully the difference and diversity which characterises contemporary British society' (Deacon and Mann, 1999, p 413). Yet others have identified the potential of agency, 'to add another texture' to 'the consideration of, and transformation of, social problems' (Orbach, 1999, p 13).

Of central importance, we have argued, is that agency theory offers an explanation of change. It illuminates and sheds light not only on the way societal change takes place but also on the capacity of individuals, acting either separately or collectively, to influence this process.

Agency is also about belief. In particular it highlights the importance of self-belief, both for service users and for those of us who work with them, in whatever capacity. Fundamentally, it suggests that we all have the ability, service users and professionals alike, to reflect, to create our own meaning, to resist where necessary the definitions imposed on us, and to contribute to change.

Ultimately, what agency theory has to offer is the basis for a new kind of hope: an optimism based on the knowledge that what shapes the lives both of service users and ourselves is not immutable, but something that, if we choose to do so, we all have the power to influence and transform.

What has been attempted in this book, however, represents what is hoped to be just the beginning of a much wider debate about the significance of agency to social work. It will be for others, if they choose to do so, to develop these ideas and take them forward.

Afterword

A few months ago, I attended a meeting of Philosophy Cafe in Leeds. The facilitator, author of at least one philosophical book himself, introduced the discussion by asking if anyone's life had been changed by philosophy. It was, I suspect, a question expecting the answer 'no', but honesty and a commitment to the ideas contained within this book forced me to put up my hand and admit that mine had.

For my life *has* been changed. Put simply, in the twenty years since I was introduced to these ideas, I have moved from being a glass half empty to a glass half full person, someone who now views life with an enthusiasm I had not previously experienced since childhood – a change that I know is largely attributable to being introduced to the ideas contained within these pages. They have affected my work, my personal life and the way I view the world. Indeed, it is the awareness of the power of these ideas, and the impact they have had on my own life that has compelled me to commit them to writing.

So, if in reading this book and learning about individual agency and its potential even one person has their life or work similarly transformed, then writing it will have proved totally worthwhile.

Liz Jeffery
4 March 2010
e.jeffery111@ntlworld.com

Bibliography

Allan, C. (2009) 'My brilliant survival guide', *Society Guardian*, 14 January.

Althusser, L. (2001 [1970]) 'Ideology and ideological state apparatuses', in *Lenin and philosophy and other essays*, New York: Monthly Review Press.

Antonovsky, A. (1979) *Health, stress and coping*. San Francisco: Jossey-Bass.

Antonovsky, A. (1988) 'Family sense of coherence and family adaptation', *Journal of Marriage and the Family*, no 50, February, pp 79–92.

Archer, M. (1982) 'Morphogenesis versus structuration: on combining structure and action', *British Journal of Sociology*, vol 33, no 4, pp 455–83.

Archer, M. (1998) *Culture and agency: The place of agency in social theory*. Cambridge: Cambridge University Press.

Archer, M. (2000) *Being human: The problem of agency*. Cambridge: Cambridge University Press.

Aries, P. (1981) *The hour of our death*. New York: Vintage Books.

Arnstein, S.R. (1969) 'A ladder of citizen participation', in *Journal of the American Planning Association*, vol 36, no 4, pp 216–24.

Babbit, S. (2001) *Artless integrity: Moral imagination, integrity and stories*. Lanham, MD: Rowman and Littlefield.

Bailey, R. and Brake, M. (eds) (1975) *Radical social work*. London: Edward Arnold.

Balbernie, R. (1999) 'Infant mental health', *Young Minds Magazine*, no 38, pp 12-15.

Banks, S. (2006) *Ethics and values in social work*. Basingstoke: Palgrave Macmillan.

Barnes, B. (2000) *Understanding agency: Social theory and responsible action*. London: Sage.

Barnes, M. (1997) *Care, communities and citizens*. London: Longham.

Barry, M. and Hallett, C. (eds.) (1998) *Social exclusion and social work*. London: Random House Press.

Bateman.T. (2006) 'Youth crime and justice: statistical 'evidence', recent trends and responses', in B. Goldson and J. Muncie (eds) *Youth crime and justice*. London: Sage.

Batsleer, J. and Humphreys, B. (eds) (2000) *Welfare, exclusion and political agency*. London: Routledge.

Bauman, Z. (1997) *Postmodernity and its discontents*. Cambridge: Polity Press.

Beck, U. (1993) *The risk society*. London: Sage.

Benjamin, A. (2005) 'Out in the lead', *The Guardian* (5 January).

Bentall, R. (1990) *Reconstructing schizophrenia*. London: Routledge.

Benton, T. (2003) 'Ian Craib', *The Guardian* (18 February).

Beresford, P., Branfield, F., Taylor, J., Brennan, M., Sartori, A., Lalani, M. and Wise, G. (2006) 'Working together for better social work education', *Social Work Education*, vol 25, no 4, pp 326–31.

Beresford, P., Adshead, L., Croft, S. and Rowe, D. (2007) *Palliative care, social work and service users: Making life possible*. London: Jessica Kingsley.

Biestek, F. (1961) *The casework relationship*, London: Allen and Unwin.

Boddy, J., Statham, J., McQuail, S., Petrie, P. and Owen, C. (2009) *Working at the 'edges' of care? European models of support for young people and families.* London: DCSF.

Bratman, M.E. (2007) *Structures of agency*, Oxford: Oxford University Press.

Brook, E. and Davis, A. (1985) *Women, the family and social work.* London: Tavistock.

Brown, C. (ed) (2001) *Recovery and wellness.* Binghamton, NY: Haworth Press.

Bunting, M. (2004) *Willing slaves.* London: HarperCollins.

Bunting, M. (2008a) 'The legacy of the pitmen', *Guardian* (7 June).

Bunting, M. (2008b) 'Happy mediums', *Guardian* (30 April).

Bunting, M. (2009) 'Forget 'clients' and 'users': public services are about people', *Guardian* (30 September).

Butler–Sloss, E. (1988) *Report of the Inquiry into Child Abuse in Cleveland.* London: HMSO.

Butrym, Z. (1976) *The nature of social work.* Basingstoke: Macmillan.

Butt, J. and Box, L. (1998) *Family centred: A study of the use of family centres by black families.* London: Race Equality Foundation.

Callinicos, A. (2004) *Making history: Agency, structure and change in social theory.* Leiden, The Netherlands: Brill Academic Publishers.

Campbell, D. (2009) *Guardian,* Letters (30 September).

Cannan, C. and Warren, C. (eds) (1997) *Social action with children and families.* London: Routledge.

Cannan, C., Berry, L. and Lyons, K. (1992) *Social work and Europe.* London: Macmillan.

Carsnaes, W. (1992) 'The agency–structure problem in foreign policy analysis', *International Studies Quarterly,* vol 36, pp 247–70.

CWDC (Children's Workforce Development Council) (2009) *Creating a world class social care workforce.* Leeds: CWDC.

Clare, A.W. (1981) *Let's talk about me: A critical examination of the new psychotherapies.* London: BBC.

Clark, C. and Dugdale, G. (2008) *Literacy changes lives: The role of literacy in offending behaviour.* London: National Literacy Trust.

Clark, J., Modgil C. and Modgil, S. (1990) *Anthony Giddens: Consensus and controversy.* London: Falmer Press.

Corrigan, P. and Leonard, P. (1978) *Social work practice under capitalism.* Basingstoke: Macmillan.

Craib, I. (1992) *Anthony Giddens.* London: Routledge.

Crockett, L. (ed.) (2002) *Agency, motivation and the life course.* Lincoln, NE: University of Nebraska Press.

CWDC (Children's Workforce Development Council) (2009) *Creating a world class social care workforce.* Leeds: CWDC.

Davies, B. (1982) 'Towards a personalist framework for radical social work education', in Bailey, R. and Lee, P. (eds) *Theory and practice in social work.* Oxford: Blackwell.

DCSF (Department for Children, Schools and Familes) (2008) *The Play Strategy.* London: DCFS.

Deacon, A. and Mann, K. (1999) 'Agency, modernity and social policy', *Journal of Social Policy*, vol 28, no 3, pp 413–35.

DfES (Department for Education and Skills) (2004) *Every child matters: Change for children*. London: DfES.

Dominelli, L. (2004) *Social work: Theory and practice for a changing profession*. Cambridge: Polity Press.

Dominelli, L. and McLeod, E. (1989) *Feminist social work*. Basingstoke: Macmillan.

Durkheim, E. (1892) 'Montesquieu's contribution to the rise of social science' (1892), in *Montesquieu and Rousseau: Forerunners of sociology*, trans. Ralph Manheim (1960), p 9, Ann Arbor, MI: University of Michigan Press.

Durkheim, E. (1895) *Rules of sociological method*. trans. W.D. Halls (1982) New York, NY: Free Press.

Dyson, A. (2004) 'The role of education in prevention', in National Evaluation of the Children's Fund, Conference Papers, 17 June.

Eliot, T.S. 'Sweeney Agonistes', in T.S. Eliot (1963) *Collected Poems, 1909–1962*. London: Faber and Faber.

Eyre, R. (2005) 'Ballot Box Blues', *Guardian* (26 March).

Fanon, F. (1952) *Black skins, white masks*. Editions du Seuil, Paris, trans. Richard Philcox (2008) New York, NY: Grove Press.

Fanon, F. (1965) *The wretched of the earth*. London: Macgibbon and Kee.

Feaver, W. (2009) 'Anyone can paint', *Guardian* (24 January).

Ferguson, H. (2003) 'Welfare, social exclusion and reflexivity', *Journal of Social Policy*, vol 32, no 2, pp 199–216.

Ferguson, I. (2008) *Reclaiming social work*. London: Sage.

Fitzpatrick, M. (2009) 'Kids in', *Guardian Review* (28 February).

Fook, J. (2002) *Critical theory and practice*. London: Sage.

Foucault, M. (1975) *Discipline and punish*. London: Allen Lane.

Foucault, M. (1981) *A history of sexuality*. London: Penguin.

Foucault, M. (2004) 'The panopticon', in D.M. Kaplan (ed) Readings in the philosophy of technology. Lanham, MD: Rowan and Littlefield.

Fransella, F. and Dalton, P. (1990) *Personal construct counselling in action*. London: Sage.

Freire, P. (1970) *The pedagogy of the oppressed*. London: Continuum Publishing Company.

Freud, S. (1900) *The interpretation of dreams*. New York, NY: Macmillan.

Freud, S. (1901) *The psychopathology of everyday life*. London: T. Fisher-Unwin.

Froggett, L. (2002) *Love, hate and welfare*. Bristol: The Policy Press.

Frost, E. and Hoggett, P. (2008) 'Human agency and social suffering', *Critical Social Policy*, vol 28, no 4, pp 438–60.

Frost, N. and Stein, M. (1989) *The politics of child welfare*. Hemel Hempstead: Harvester Wheatsheaf.

Frost, N., Lloyd, A. and Jeffery, L. (2003) *The RHP companion to family support*. Lyme Regis: Russell House Publishing.

Fudge, S. (2009) 'Reconciling structure with agency', *Critical Social Policy*, vol 29, no 1, pp 53–76.

Garfinkel, H. (1967) *Studies in ethnomethodology*. Englewood Cliffs, NJ: Prentice-Hall.

Garland, R. (2001) *The culture of control: Crime and social order in contemporary society*. Chicago: University of Chicago Press.

Gerth, H.H. and Wright Mills, C. (1948) *From Max Weber: Essays in sociology*. International Library of Sociology, London: Routledge and Kegan Paul.

Giddens, A. (1979) *Central problems in social theory*. Basingstoke: Macmillan.

Giddens, A. (1984) *The constitution of society: Outline of the theory of structuration*. Cambridge: Polity Press.

Giddens, A. (1991) *Modernity and self-identity*. Palo Alto, CA: Stanford University Press.

Gill, T. (1995) *Playing for local government: How local authorities can enhance their corporate strategies and service planning by supporting children's play*. London: National Children's Bureau.

Goffman, E. (1962) *Asylums*. Chicago, IL: Aldine Publishing Company.

Goldson, B. and Muncie, J. (eds) (2006) *Youth crime and justice*. London: Sage.

Gould, M. (2008) 'Liberation theory', in *Society Guardian* (30 January).

Groskop, V. (2009) 'Escape from the past' (Interview with B. Cyrulnik) *Guardian* (18 April).

Halmos, P. (1965) *The faith of the counsellors*. London: Constable.

Harre, R. (1979) *Social being*. Oxford: Blackwell.

Harre, R. (1983) *Personal being*. Oxford: Blackwell.

Harre, R. and Secord, P.F. (1972) *The explanation of social behaviour*. Oxford: Blackwell.

Hendry, J. (1997) *An alternative model of agency theory and its application to corporate governance*. Cambridge: Judge Institute of Management Studies.

Hobbes, T. (1998 [1651]) *Leviathan*. Oxford: Oxford University Press.

Holman, B. (1998) *Faith in the poor*. Oxford: Lion Books.

Hoggett, P. (2001) 'Agency, rationality and social policy', *Journal of Social Policy*, vol 30, no 1, pp 37–56.

Horne, M. (1987) *Values in social work*. Aldershot: Wildwood House/Community Care.

Howe, D. (1987) *An Introduction to Social Work Theory*. Aldershot: Ashgate/Community Care.

Hudson, A. (1989) 'Challenging perspectives: feminism, gender and social work', in M. Langan and P. Lee (1989) *Radical social work today*. London: Unwin, Hyman.

Hudson, J. and Galloway, B. (1996) *Family group conferences: Perspectives on policy and practice*. Annandale, NSW: Federation Press.

Humphries, B. (2000) 'Resources for hope', in J. Batsleer and B. Humphreys (eds) *Welfare, exclusion and political agency*. London: Routledge.

Huxley, A. (1954) *The doors of perception*. London: Chatto and Windus.

Jencks, C. (1994) *The homeless*. Cambridge, MA: Harvard University Press. Cambridge, MA:

Jenkins, S. (2010) 'Straw has left justice to the tender mercies of the press', *Guardian* (9 March).

Johnson, M. (2009) 'Prisoners are ready for a taste of democracy', in *Society Guardian* (16 September).

Jones, C. (1983) *State social work and the working class*. Basingstoke: Macmillan.

Jones, C. (1996) 'Anti-intellectualism and the peculiarities of British social work education', in N. Parton (ed) *Social theory, social change and social work*. London: Routledge.

Jones, G. S. (1971) *Outcast*. London: Clarendon Press.

Jones, H. (ed) (1975) *Towards a new social work*. London: Routledge and Kegan Paul.

Jones, S. (2010) 'You're stigmatised if you live on a council estate', *Guardian* (27 January).

Jordan, B. (2003) 'Choice, independence and well-being: Social work should challenge the contradiction', unpublished paper delivered to University of Nottingham conference, Affecting our value base.

Jung, C. (1912) *Psychology of the unconscious*. trans. B.M. Hinkle (1916) London: Kegan Paul Trench Trubner.

Jung, C. and Baynes, H.G. (1921) *Psychological types or, The psychology of individualisation*. London: Kegan Paul Trench Trubner (Collected works, vol 6).

Kaplan, D.M. (ed) (2004) *Readings in the philosophy of technology*. Lanham, MD: Rowan and Littlefield.

Kelly, G.A. (1955) *The psychology of personal constructs*. New York: Norton.

Kirby, P., Lanyon, C., Cronin K. and Sinclair, R. (2003) *Building a culture of participation*. London: Department for Education and Skills.

Kraemer, S. (1999) 'Promoting resilience: Changing concepts of parenting and child care', *International Journal of Child and Family Welfare*, vol 3, pp 273–87.

Kubler-Ross (1975) (ed) *Death: The final stage of growth*. Upper Saddle River, NJ: Prentice Hall.

Laing, R.D. (1967) *The politics of experience and the bird of paradise*. London: Penguin.

Langan, M. and Lee, P. (1989) *Radical social work today*. London: Unwin Hyman.

Layard, R. (2005) *Happiness: Lessons from a new science*. London: Allen Lane.

Le Grand, J. (2003) *Motivation, agency and public policy*. Oxford: Oxford University Press.

Leonard, P. (1984) *Personality and ideology*. Basingstoke: Macmillan.

Lindley, R. (1986) *Autonomy*. Basingstoke: Macmillan.

Lister, R. (1998) 'In from the margins: Citizenship, inclusion and exclusion', in M. Barry and C. Hallett(eds) *Social exclusion and social work*. London: Random House Publications.

Lister, R. (2004) *Poverty*. Cambridge: Polity Press.

Lorenz, W. (1994) *Social work in a changing Europe*. London: Routledge.

Lowe, E.J. (2008) *Personal agency: The metaphysics of mind and action*. Oxford: Oxford University Press.

Lukes, S. (1974) *Power: A radical view*. Basingstoke: Macmillan.

Malek, A.A. (1963) 'Orientalism in crisis', *Diogenes*, vol 44, pp 107–8.

Mann, K. (1985) 'The making of a claiming class: the neglect of agency in analyses of the welfare state', *Critical Social Policy*, vol 5, no 15, pp 62–74.

Marqusee, M. (2009) 'I don't need a war to fight my cancer – I need empowering as a patient', *Guardian* (30 December).

Marx, K. (1852) *The 18th Brumaire of Louis Bonaparte*. New York, NY: Die Revolution.

Marx, K. and Engels, F. (1848) *The Communist Manifesto*. London: Duetsche Landoner Zeitung.

Mayer, J. and Timms, N. (1970) *The client speaks*. London: Routledge and Kegan Paul.

McSmith, A. (2008) 'How do you sell the housing estate from hell?', *Independent* (20 October).

Mental Health Foundation (1999) *Brighter futures: Promoting children and young people's mental health*. London: Mental Health Foundation.

Mickel, A. (2009) 'Exclusive survey reveals workforce that is dedicated but less than happy', *Community Care* (30 July).

Morris, N. (2006) 'Blair's "frenzied law making": a new offence for every day spent in office', *Independent* (16 August).

Muir, H. (2005) 'Deliberately demoralising', *Guardian* (18 May).

National Play Strategy (2008) *Department for Children, Schools and Families*. London: DCSF.

Newman, T. (2002) *Promoting resilience: A review of effective strategies for child care services*. London: Barnardo's.

Obama, B. (2007) *The audacity of hope*. Edinburgh: Canongate Books.

Oliver, M. (2004) 'If I had a hammer: the social model in action', in J. Swain, S. French, C. Barnes and C. Thomas (eds) *Disabling barriers: Enabling environments*. London: Sage.

O'Neill, O. (2002) *A question of trust*. Cambridge: Cambridge University Trust.

Orbach, S. (1999) 'Listening to your analyst', *London School of Economics Magazine*, vol 11, no 1, pp 12–13.

Page, R. and Clark, G.A. (eds) (1977) *Who cares? Young people in care speak out*. London: NCB.

Parsons, T. (1937) *The structure of social action*. Maidenhead: McGraw Hill.

Parton, N. (ed) (1996) *Social theory, social change and social work*. London: Routledge.

Parton, N. (2008) 'Changes in the form of knowledge in social work: from the "social" to the "informational"', *British Journal of Social Work*, vol 38, no 2, pp 253–69.

Parton, N. and O'Byrne, P. (2000) *Constructive social work: Towards a new practice*. Basingstoke: Palgrave Macmillan.

Pearson, G. (1975) 'The politics of uncertainty', in H. Jones (ed) *Towards a new social work*. London: Routledge and Kegan Paul.

Petrie, P., Boddy, J., Cameron, C., Wigfall, V. and Simon, A. (2006) *Working with children in care: European perspectives*. Maidenhead: Open University Press.

Philp, M. (1979) 'Notes on the form of knowledge in social work', *Sociological Review*, vol 27, no 1, pp 83–111.

Piaget, J. (1928) *The child's conception of his world*. London: Routledge and Kegan Paul.

Pickett, K.E. and Wilkinson, R.G. (2000) 'Child poverty in perspective: an overview of child well-being in rich countries', Florence: *Innocenti Research Centre*, UNICEF.

Plant, R. (1970) *Social and moral theory in casework*. London: Routledge and Kegan Paul.

Plant, R. (1983) *Hegel: An introduction*. Oxford: Blackwell.

Postle, K. and Beresford, P. (2007) 'Capacity building and the reconception of political participation: a role for social care workers?', *British Journal of Social Work*, no 37, pp 143–58.

Power, M. (1997) *The audit society: Rituals of verification*. Oxford: Oxford University Press.

Prime Minister's Strategy Unit, Department of Work and Pensions, Department of Health, Department for Education and Skills, Office of the Deputy Prime Minister (2005) *Improving the life chances of disabled people*. London: The Stationery Office.

PSSRU (Personal Social Services Research Unit) (2008) *Individual budgets evaluation*. York: PSSRU.

Riessman, C.K. (1989) 'Life events, meaning and narrative: The case of infidelity and divorce', *Social Science & Medicine* (29), pp 743-51.

Robertson, J. and Robertson, J. (1989) *Separation and the very young*. London: Free Association Books.

Roche, B. (2003) Paper presented at 'Affirming our values' conference, Nottingham.

Rogers, C. (1961) *On becoming a person*. New York: Mariner Books.

Romme, M. and Escher, S. (eds)(1993) *Accepting voices*. London: MIND Publications.

Rose, S., Lewontin, R.C and Kamin, L.J (1984) *Not in our genes*. London: Penguin.

Rousseau, E. (1762) *The social contract*. Amsterdam: Marc Michel Rey.

Rowe, D. (2008) *Guardian*, Letters (9 April).

Rusbridger, A. (2009) 'Democracy in the decade of Google', *Guardian* (17 October).

Russell, J. (2009) 'Where, they ask, is all the gratitude? Well, it's the experience, stupid', *Guardian* (15 July).

Rutter, M. (1990) 'Psychosocial resilience and protective mechanisms', in J. Rolf, A.S. Masten, D. Cicchetti, K.H. Nuechterlein and S. Weintraub (eds) *Risk and protective factors in the development of psychopathology*. New York: Press Syndicate, University of Cambridge.

Rutter, M. (2006) 'Promotion of resilience in the face of adversity', in A. Clarke-Stewart and J. Dunn (eds) *Families count: Effects on adolescent and child development*. Cambridge: Cambridge University Press.

Said, E. (1978) *Orientalism*. New York, NY: Random House USA.

Said, E. (1994) *Orientalism.* (25th Anniversary Edition). New York, NY: Vintage Books, Random House.

Sands, R. (1996) 'The elusiveness of identity in social work practice with women,' *Clinical Social Work Journal*, vol 24, no 2, pp 167–86.

SCIE (Social Care Institute for Excellence) (2009) 'Proven practice: the evidence base for social care practice', *Community Care* (16 April).

Segal, L. (1987) *Is the future female?* London: Virago.

Seligman, M.E.P. (1975) *Helplessness: On depression, development and death.* New York: Freeman/Times Books.

Sen, A. (1999a) *Development as freedom.* Oxford: Oxford University Press.

Sen, A. (1999b) 'Reason before identity', *Romanes lectures.* Oxford: Oxford University Press.

Skynner, R. and Cleese, J. (1983) *Families and how to survive them.* London: Methuen.

Simonton, C. (1978) *Getting well again.* Los Angeles, CA: J.P. Tarcher Inc. (unavailable).

Simpson, G. and Price, V. (2007) *Transforming society? Social work and sociology.* Bristol: The Policy Press.

Smith, C. (2000) 'Social work as rights talk', in J. Harris, L. Froggett and I. Paylor (eds) *Reclaiming social work: The Southport papers*, vol 1, Birmingham: Venture Press.

Smith, M.K. (2009) 'Social pedagogy' in *The encyclopaedia of informal education* (www.infed.org/biblio/b-socped.htm).

Smith, R. (2008) *Social work and power.* Basingstoke: Palgrave Macmillan.

Stedman-Jones, G. (1971) *Outcast London.* Oxford: Clarendon Press.

Stenner, P. and Taylor, D. (2008) 'Psychosocial welfare: reflections on an emerging field', *Critical Social Policy*, vol 28, no 4, pp 415–37.

Stone, E. (1988) *Black sheep and kissing cousins: How our family stories shape us.* New York: Time Books.

Stones, R. (2005) *Structuration theory.* Basingstoke: Palgrave Macmillan.

Sylva, K. (1977) 'Play and Learning', in B. Tizard and D. Harvey (eds) *Biology of play.* London: Heinemann.

Tan, J.E.C., Jarvis, P., Conway, P. and Hall, K. (2008) *Evaluation of 'reading matters' (executive summary).* Leeds: Leeds Metropolitan University.

Tatchell, P. (1986) *AIDS: A guide to survival.* Kalispell, MT: Heretic Books.

Thatcher, M. (1987) 'Aids, education and the year 2001!', Interview, *Woman's Own* (31 October) pp 8-10.

Thompson, E.P. (1963) *The making of the English working class.* London: Gollancz.

Thompson, E.P. (1978) *The poverty of theory.* London: Merlin.

Titmuss, R. (1958) *Essays on the welfare state.* London: Allen and Unwin.

Titterton, M. (1992) 'Managing threats to welfare: the search for a new paradigm of welfare', *Journal of Social Policy*, vol 21, no 1, pp 1–23.

Tolstoy, L. (1878) *Anna Karenina.* Moscow (1878) and London: Penguin Classics, (2001).

UNICEF (2007) *The declaration on child well-being.* London: UNICEF.

Utting, W. (1998) *People like us.* London: The Stationery Office.

Walrond–Skinner, S. (1976) *Family therapy: The treatment of natural systems.* Lavenham: Lavenham Press.

Walsh, D.F. (1998) 'Structure/agency', in C. Jenks (ed) *Core sociological dichotomies.* London: Sage.

White, M. and Epston, D. (1990) *Narrative means to therapeutic ends.* New York: W.W. Norton.

Wilkinson, R.G. and Pickett, K. (2009) *The spirit level.* London: Allen Lane.

Williams, F. (1996) 'Postmodernism, feminism and the question of difference', in N. Parton (ed) *Social theory, social change and social work.* London: Routledge.

Williams, F. (1999) 'Good enough principles for welfare,' *Journal of Social Policy,* vol 28, no 4, pp 667–87.

Williams, F., Popay, J. and Oakley, A. (1999) *Welfare research: A critical review and new synthesis.* London: University College London Press.

Winn, M. (2002) *The plug-in drug: Television, computers and family life.* New York: Penguin.

Woodroofe, K. (1962) *From charity to social work.* London: Routledge and Kegan Paul.

Websites

Faith–Based Regeneration Network (www.fbrn.org.uk)
The Who Cares? Trust (www.thewhocarestrust.org.uk)

Index

Laing, R.D. 17
Leonard, P. 20, 84
life-planning and reflexivity 65
Lister, Ruth 27, 68-9
literacy skills
  illiteracy and offending 82-3
  Reading Matters initiative 81, 83-4
'looked-after' children
  People like us report 71
  and service-user movement 63-4, 84
  and social pedagogy approach 88
Lorenz, W. 87
Lukes, S. 29, 59

M

Machiavelli, Niccolò 58-9
McLeod, E. 38
Malek, A.A. 69
managerialism and social workers 89-90, 100
  impact on training 101
  and loss of individual voice 90-1
Mann, Kirk 6, 25, 27, 29, 105
marginalisation 30
  and binary approach 29, 49, 57, 70
  and 'the other' 69-72, 73, 80-1
Marqusee, M. 55
Marx, Karl 9-10, 102
Mayer, J. 62
meaning: individual meaning 97
measurement *see* scientific measurement
media and voice of social work 91
mental health
  and 'sense of coherence' 39-40, 49, 65
  social work with people with mental health
    problems 48-50
    relationship with social worker 51-2
    subjective view from social work 48-9
    'user-controlled' research 63
modernist approach to social work 26-7
Montessori, Maria 41
moral nature of social work 25, 52
  need for ethical focus in training 101-2

N

narrative and identity 14, 49-50, 65-6, 85, 97
national Play Strategy 41
National Voice 63, 64
negative agency and offending 43-4, 50-1, 99
negative freedom 17
Newman, T. 39
non-decision-making 59
norms *see* social norms

O

Obama, Barack 82
objective social work approaches 18, 19-22, 23
  objectification of service users 30, 31, 56
    importance of relationship with users
      99-100

labelling of social groups and
    empowerment 56-7, 58, 70-1
  and loss of individual voice 90-1
  and managerial methods 89-90, 100
  as 'the other' 30, 69-71, 72, 89
  as passive victims 20, 21, 22, 29, 57, 72
  resistance and individual meaning 97
  and paradox of social work 24
O'Byrne, P. 39, 47, 52, 96
offenders
  and narrative identity construction 65-6, 97
  as 'the other' in punitive climate 70
  pre-sentence report writing 24, 42
  self-belief and identity 98
  service-user involvement 64
  see also young offenders
Oliver, M. 64
O'Neill, O. 89
optimistic approaches 25, 30, 94, 104
Orbach, Susie 27, 105
Orientalism 69
'other, the' 53, 69-72, 73
  and educational system 80-1
  Fanon and colonisation 76, 80
  and feminist approaches 21
  and labelling of social groups 45, 70-1
  and objectification of service users 30, 69-71, 72, 89
  resistance to 'othering' 71, 72, 73, 84-5, 97, 98

P

parent empowerment 56-7, 67
Parsons, Talcott 10-11
participation and service users 52, 53, 73
  and power 61-9
  unintended consequences 60
  voice of service users 92-3
Parton, N. 23, 39, 47, 52, 96
patients as co-producers 67
Pearson, G. 23, 23-4, 28
People like us report 71
performance management in social work 30, 89-90, 100, 101
personal construct approach 42-3
personalisation agenda 67
Petrie, P. 87
philanthropy and origins of social work 15, 16, 23
Philp, Mark 5, 15, 18, 48, 56, 90, 96-7
  'form of knowledge' 23-5
Piaget, Jean 12
Plant, Raymond 5, 16-18, 24, 25, 96
play and work with children 40-1, 50
political engagement and social work 88-93
Poor Laws 15, 16
Popay, J. 63
positive freedom 17
Postle, K. 64, 89

self-realisation 8
Sen, Amartya 75, 82, 88, 92, 101, 102
  education and agency 78-9, 80
  freedom and agency 78-9, 80, 85-6, 94, 96
'sense of coherence' 39-40, 49, 51, 65, 85
service provision: co-production 67-8
service user involvement 53, 62-5, 84
service users and agency 2-3
  client-centred approach 18-19, 22, 30-1, 38, 57-8, 60, 89
  negative and positive freedoms 17
  as 'the other' 69-72, 73
  participation
    and dying 52, 53, 54-5, 60, 73
    empowerment issues 55-61, 73
    and power 61-9, 73
    service provision and co-production 67-8
    service-user involvement 62-5
    voice of service users 92-3
  and social workers 33-52
    children and young people as service users 40-4, 50-1
    empowerment of service users 36-7, 38
    social pedagogy as approach 87, 103
    and structural oppression 36-7, 44, 48, 49, 58, 60
    views of own agency 29, 45-6
  see also experience of service users and social work
Shaping Our Lives 63
Simonton, C. 55
Simpson, G. 102
'situated subjectivity' 49
Smith, C. 61
Smith, R. 58, 66, 71
social class
  arts and empowerment 72
  and development of social work discourse 23
  and power 11-12
  and structural change 12-13
  and systems 11
social control and role of social worker 46, 51
social enquiry reports 24
social exclusion
  and binary approach 29, 49, 57, 70
  and failure of education system 83
  and lack of agency 25, 26, 27, 45, 69, 71
  and objectification of service users 30, 69-71, 72
  and 'othering' of marginalised groups 69-72, 73, 80-1
  theory and social work paradox 23, 24
social groups
  dominant and subordinate groups 11-12, 12-13, 64, 70
  empowerment of groups not individuals 56-7, 58
  see also labelling of social groups; marginalisation

social norms 10-11, 13, 17, 29
  see also 'other, the'
social pedagogy 43, 86-8, 103
social policy: resistance to agency of poor 27
social production of power 59
'social suffering' 45
social welfare
  dual role 23, 28
  and internationalist perspective 84-6
  origins of welfare state 15-16
social work
  agency as way forward 95-106
    and training in social care 101-5
  as art 100
  dual role 23, 28
  internationalist perspective 75-84
  political context 88-93
    mediating role 90-1, 96-7
    undermining of profession 88-90
  and power 46-7, 48, 61-9
    theories of power 57-61
    unintended consequences 14, 60
  target-driven culture and agency 30, 89, 100
  theoretical influences 14-29
    and dilemma of social work 17-18
    and foundations of social work 15, 23
    and paradox of social work 23-4
    subjective and objective approaches 18-25, 56, 57, 58, 70-1, 72, 96-7
    theories of power 57-61
  training and future implications 101-5
  see also social welfare; social workers
social workers 1, 2
  conflict and rivalry between 103
  and political context
    mediating and disseminating role 90-2, 96-7
    undermining of work of 88-90
  and service users 33-52
    attitudes of social workers to work and clients 34-5, 99, 104
    mediating role as agents of change 37, 38-9, 44, 48, 51-2, 90, 91-2, 96-7
    relationship and agency 31, 51-2, 90, 99-100
    and social pedagogy approach 87, 103
    and structural oppression 36-7, 44, 48, 49, 58, 60
    and unconscious power 60
    work with children and young people 40-4, 50-1
  social control role 46, 51
  see also training in social work
society: theoretical perspectives 8-14
sociology and agency theory 1, 5, 8-9
  and social care training 102
solution-focused therapy 47
state
  dual role of social work 23, 28